HONOURING VIRTUE

RECOGNIZING ETHICAL EXCELLENCE IN EDUCATION

DR. MINAKSHI BANSAL

DEDICATION

This book is dedicated to all the educators who inspire ethical excellence through their unwavering commitment to integrity, fairness, and compassion. To the students who strive to make ethical choices, and to the parents and community members who support and nurture these values. Your dedication and passion are the heart of our educational system, and together, you make the world a better place, one virtuous act at a time.

❦❦❦

Contents

Contents

Prayer

"Om Bhadram Karnebhih Shrinuyama Devah

Bhadram Pashyemakshabhiryajatrah

Sthirairangais Tushtuvamsastanubhih

Vyashema Devahitam Yadayuh

Svasti Na Indro Vriddhashravah

Svasti Nah Pusha Vishwavedah

Svasti Nastarkshyo Arishtanemih

Svasti No Brihaspatir Dadhatu

Om Shantih Shantih Shantih"

This mantra is a prayer for universal well-being, invoking the blessings of various deities for protection, health, and happiness. It emphasizes the importance of experiencing the auspicious through all senses and living a life aligned with divine purpose. The repetition of "Shantih" at the end signifies a deep desire for peace in the individual, the environment, and the universe at large. This mantra is often recited as a prayer for peace, prosperity, and the physical and spiritual well-being of all beings.

❧❧❧

About The Author

This book represents the culmination of extensive research and meticulous analysis, incorporating a diverse range of sources, including numerous books, scholarly studies, and personal experiences. Additionally, I have scoured various websites to gather relevant information and data essential for the compilation of this work. I have taken every precaution to ensure the accuracy of the information presented and have diligently cited all sources to acknowledge their contributions.

From her earliest days, Minakshi was distinguished by an insatiable appetite for reading. Her literary universe was inhabited by characters and narratives that spanned ethical tales, motivational and inspirational stories, and the mythic parables imbued with life lessons. This voracious reading habit was not merely for personal edification but was driven by a desire to distill and disseminate the essence of these narratives to foster the development of students and peers alike. She was particularly captivated by the lives and teachings of historical figures and spiritual leaders such as Adi Shankaracharya, Swami Vivekananda, Dr. APJ Abdul Kalam, Mahamana Pandit Madan Mohan Malviya, Mahatma Gandhi, Sardar Vallabhai Patel, and Vinoba Bhave, among others. Their philosophies and life stories fueled her ambition to embody their ideals of resilience, selflessness, and relentless pursuit of knowledge.

Dr. Minakshi's academic and practical engagement with psychology has been equally noteworthy. As a research scholar, her focus has been on exploring the intricate tapestry of the human psyche, aiming to unlock the potential for psychological well-being and societal harmony. Her scholarly work is complemented by her active involvement in social work, where she employs her academic insights to make tangible differences in the lives of the underprivileged. Her endeavours in social work are characterized by an innovative approach that combines traditional wisdom with contemporary psychological practices to address the multifaceted challenges faced by these communities.

Her artistic talents, another facet of her diverse capabilities, are not merely a personal passion but also serve as a medium through which she communicates and connects with others. Her art, rich in symbolism and emotional depth, reflects her philosophical inquiries and social concerns, offering viewers a glimpse into the breadth of her intellect and the depth of her compassion.

In addition to her contributions to the arts and social sciences, Dr. Minakshi has embraced the healing arts of Pranic Healing, mastering the techniques developed by Master Choa Kok Sui. This practice, which focuses on the manipulation of Prana or life energy to heal the body and aura, has been both a personal journey of discovery and a means through which she extends her healing touch to others. Her proficiency in Pranic Healing is complemented by her advocacy and teaching of various forms of meditation aimed at rejuvenation, personal betterment, and the cultivation of harmony within individuals and communities alike.

Dr. Minakshi's life is a narrative of relentless pursuit, not just of personal achievement but of the upliftment and empowerment of society at large. Her diverse interests and talents—spanning the arts, literature, psychology, and the healing practices—converge on a singular path of service. She embodies the spirit of the luminaries who inspired her, channelling their legacy through her actions and teachings. Through her books, art, and social initiatives, she continues to inspire a new generation to embark on their own journeys of self-discovery, resilience, and altruism.

Her commitment to social betterment, particularly her focus on uplifting underprivileged children, reflects a deep understanding of the transformative potential of education and personal development. By integrating her knowledge of psychology, her artistic sensibilities, and her healing practices, Dr. Bansal has developed a holistic approach to social work that addresses both the immediate needs and the long-term well-being of the communities she serves.

As an author, Dr. Minakshi's writings offer a blend of inspirational insights, practical wisdom, and reflective contemplations drawn from her extensive reading and life experiences. Her books serve as a guide for those seeking to navigate the complexities of life with grace, resilience, and purpose. Through her narratives, she extends an invitation to her readers to explore the depths of their own potential and to contribute meaningfully to the collective well-being of society.

In Dr. Minakshi Bansal, we find a remarkable synthesis of the artist, the scholar, the healer, and the social activist. Her life's work stands as a beacon of hope and a source of inspiration for individuals seeking to make a difference in the world. Her story is a compelling reminder of the power of individual action, rooted in compassion and driven by a profound commitment to the betterment of humanity. Dr. Minakshi's legacy is not just in the tangible outcomes of her efforts but in the enduring spirit of inquiry, empathy, and service that she embodies.

ᐅᐅᐅ

Preface

As an educator with years of experience and a deep commitment to fostering ethical excellence in education, I am both honored and excited to present this book. Throughout my career, I have encountered countless moments that have underscored the importance of ethical behavior in the educational sphere. These experiences have shaped my understanding of what it means to be an educator and have driven me to explore the profound impact that ethics can have on the lives of students, teachers, and the broader community. This book is a culmination of my reflections, observations, and research, aimed at highlighting the critical role of ethics in education and offering insights into how we can nurture ethical excellence within our schools.

From the very beginning of my journey as an educator, I have been struck by the profound responsibility that comes with the role. Educators are not merely conveyors of knowledge; we are also role models, mentors, and guides who shape the character and values of our students. The decisions we make, the behaviors we exhibit, and the standards we uphold have a lasting impact on the young minds entrusted to our care. Recognizing this responsibility, I have always strived to lead by example, demonstrating integrity, fairness, respect, and empathy in all my interactions. It is through these daily acts of ethical behavior that we can inspire our students to adopt similar values and principles.

One of the fundamental lessons I have learned is that ethical excellence in education is not a destination but a continuous journey. It requires ongoing reflection, self-awareness, and a commitment to personal and professional growth. As educators, we must constantly evaluate our actions and decisions, seeking to align them with our core ethical principles. This process of reflection is not always easy, as it often involves confronting our own biases, mistakes, and limitations. However, it is through this introspection that we can grow as individuals and professionals, ultimately becoming more effective in our roles and more impactful in the lives of our students.

A key theme that emerges throughout this book is the importance of creating a supportive and inclusive environment within our schools. Ethical excellence cannot flourish in isolation; it thrives in a culture where trust, respect, and collaboration are prioritized. This means fostering positive relationships between students, teachers, administrators, and the broader community. It means valuing diversity and inclusivity, recognizing and celebrating the unique backgrounds and perspectives that each individual brings to the table. It means creating spaces where all members of the school community feel valued, heard, and supported. By cultivating such an environment, we lay the foundation for ethical behavior to take root and grow.

The role of leadership in promoting ethical excellence is another critical aspect explored in this book. School leaders, whether principals, administrators, or senior teachers, play a pivotal role in setting the tone and shaping the culture of their institutions. Ethical leadership involves not only making decisions that are fair and just but also modeling the behaviors and attitudes that we wish to see in our students and staff. It requires a commitment to transparency, accountability, and inclusivity. Leaders must be willing to engage in difficult conversations, address ethical dilemmas head-on, and provide support and guidance to those they lead. Through their actions, ethical leaders can inspire and motivate others to uphold the highest standards of integrity and ethical behavior.

The integration of ethics into the curriculum is another vital component of fostering ethical excellence. Ethics should not be treated as an add-on or an afterthought but as an integral part of the educational experience. This involves embedding ethical discussions and considerations into all subject areas, encouraging students to think critically about the ethical dimensions of the topics they study. It means creating opportunities for students to engage with real-world ethical dilemmas, allowing them to practice ethical reasoning and decision-making in a safe and supportive environment. By doing so, we help students develop the skills and habits necessary to navigate the complex moral landscape of the modern world.

One of the most rewarding aspects of my work has been witnessing the growth and development of my students as they grapple with ethical issues and strive to act with integrity. These moments have reinforced my belief in the power of education to shape not only minds but also hearts and characters. I have seen students rise to the challenge of ethical dilemmas, demonstrating empathy, fairness, and courage in their actions. I have seen them support and uplift one another, creating a positive and inclusive school culture. These experiences have been a source of inspiration and motivation, reminding me of the profound impact that ethical education can have on individuals and communities.

The involvement of parents and the broader community is also essential in promoting ethical excellence in education. Parents are the primary educators of their children, and their values and behaviors have a significant influence on their development. Schools must actively engage with parents, fostering open communication and collaboration to ensure that ethical principles are reinforced at home and in the community. This partnership can take many forms, from parent-teacher conferences and workshops to community service projects and cultural events. By working together, schools and families can create a cohesive and supportive environment that nurtures ethical behavior and values.

As we navigate the digital age, the ethical challenges we face have become more complex and multifaceted. Technology has transformed the way we communicate, learn, and interact, bringing with it new ethical considerations related to privacy, security, and digital literacy. It is essential for educators to guide students in understanding the ethical implications of their online behavior, promoting responsible use of technology and critical thinking about digital content. By addressing these challenges head-on, we can prepare students to navigate the digital world with integrity and respect for others.

Throughout this book, I have drawn on a variety of real-life examples and case studies to illustrate the principles and practices of ethical excellence in education. These stories highlight the successes and challenges of educators and institutions that have committed to fostering ethical behavior. They provide valuable insights and lessons that can inform and inspire our own efforts to promote ethical excellence. By learning from these examples, we can better understand the practical implications of ethical decision-making and develop strategies for addressing the ethical dilemmas we encounter in our work.

Ultimately, the path forward for ethical excellence in education requires a collective commitment from all members of the educational community. It involves embracing a shared vision of what it means to be an ethical educator, student, and leader. It means working together to create environments where integrity, fairness, respect, and empathy are prioritized and where all individuals feel valued and supported. It means recognizing that ethical excellence is not a destination but a continuous journey that requires ongoing reflection, growth, and collaboration.

As we move forward, I am filled with hope and optimism for the future of education. I believe in the power of ethical education to transform lives, build strong communities, and create a better world. I am inspired by the dedication and passion of my fellow educators, who tirelessly work to promote ethical behavior and values in their schools. I am encouraged by the resilience and determination of students, who strive to act with integrity and make positive contributions to their communities. Together, we can continue to build on the foundation of ethical excellence, creating educational environments that foster not only academic success but also moral and ethical growth. •

In writing this book, my goal has been to share my insights and experiences, to highlight the importance of ethical excellence in education, and to offer practical guidance for educators, leaders, and policymakers. I hope that this book serves as a valuable resource and a source of inspiration for all those who are committed to promoting ethical behavior and values in their schools. By working together and embracing the principles of ethical excellence, we can create a brighter and more just future for all students.

Dr. Minakshi Bansal
Social Activist
Ahmedabad, Gujarat, Bharat

ONE

Introduction: The Importance of Ethical Excellence in Education

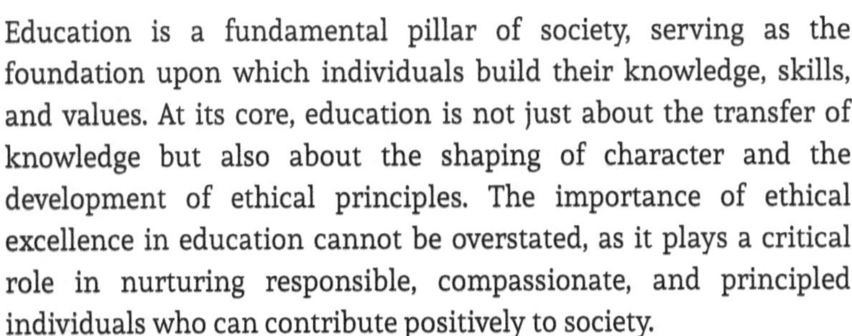

Education is a fundamental pillar of society, serving as the foundation upon which individuals build their knowledge, skills, and values. At its core, education is not just about the transfer of knowledge but also about the shaping of character and the development of ethical principles. The importance of ethical excellence in education cannot be overstated, as it plays a critical role in nurturing responsible, compassionate, and principled individuals who can contribute positively to society.

Ethical excellence in education involves the commitment to uphold and promote moral values such as integrity, honesty, fairness, respect, and responsibility. These values form the bedrock of a just and harmonious society. When educators emphasize ethical behavior and lead by example, they instill these values in their students, creating a ripple effect that extends far beyond the classroom. This process begins with educators themselves, who must embody the virtues they wish to impart to their students. The behavior and attitudes of teachers have a profound impact on students, influencing their perception of right and wrong and shaping their future actions.

Integrity, a cornerstone of ethical excellence, demands that educators remain honest and transparent in their interactions with students, colleagues, and the wider community. Integrity fosters trust, a crucial element in any educational environment. When students trust their teachers, they are more likely to engage actively in their learning and feel secure in expressing their thoughts and ideas. Trust also encourages open communication, allowing for constructive feedback and the resolution of conflicts in a respectful and fair manner.

Honesty is closely linked to integrity and is essential in creating a culture of trust and respect. Educators must model honesty in all aspects of their professional conduct, from grading and assessment to interactions with students and parents. When students observe their teachers being truthful and transparent, they are more likely to adopt these behaviors themselves. Honesty also plays a vital role in academic integrity, where the emphasis on original work and the proper acknowledgment of sources fosters a culture of respect for intellectual property and the efforts of others.

Fairness is another critical aspect of ethical excellence in education. It involves treating all students equitably, providing equal opportunities for learning and growth, and ensuring that no student is unfairly disadvantaged. Fairness requires educators to be aware of and address their biases, striving to create an inclusive environment where every student feels valued and respected. This commitment to fairness extends to the design and implementation of assessments, where the goal is to accurately measure each student's abilities and achievements without prejudice or favoritism.

Respect is fundamental to ethical behavior and is crucial in the educational context. Respect involves recognizing and valuing the inherent dignity and worth of every individual, regardless of their background, abilities, or beliefs. Educators who demonstrate respect for their students create a positive and supportive learning environment where students feel safe, valued, and motivated to succeed. Respectful interactions also promote a sense of community and belonging, which are essential for students' social and emotional well-being.

Responsibility is another key value that underpins ethical excellence in education. Educators have a responsibility to their students, their profession, and society as a whole. This responsibility includes providing high-quality education, fostering a love of learning, and preparing students to become responsible, engaged citizens. It also involves maintaining professional standards, engaging in continuous professional development, and contributing to the advancement of the educational field. When educators take their responsibilities seriously, they set a powerful example for their students, encouraging them to take responsibility for their own learning and actions.

The promotion of ethical excellence in education also involves creating a culture of accountability. Accountability means holding oneself and others responsible for their actions and ensuring that ethical standards are consistently upheld. In an educational context, this includes being accountable for the fairness and accuracy of assessments, the effectiveness of teaching methods, and the overall well-being of students. Accountability also involves addressing ethical breaches promptly and fairly, whether they involve academic dishonesty, discrimination, or other forms of misconduct. By fostering a culture of accountability, educators help to maintain the integrity and credibility of the educational system.

Compassion and empathy are essential components of ethical excellence in education. Compassion involves understanding and responding to the needs and challenges of others, while empathy involves putting oneself in another's shoes and experiencing their feelings and perspectives. Educators who demonstrate compassion and empathy create a supportive and nurturing environment where students feel understood and cared for. These qualities are particularly important in addressing the diverse needs of students, including those who may be struggling academically, socially, or emotionally. By showing compassion and empathy, educators help to build strong, positive relationships with their students, which are essential for effective teaching and learning.

The impact of ethical excellence in education extends far beyond the classroom. When students are taught and guided by ethically exemplary educators, they are more likely to develop into principled, responsible adults who contribute positively to society. Ethical education helps to cultivate a sense of moral responsibility, encouraging students to consider the impact of their actions on others and to strive for the greater good. This sense of moral responsibility is essential in addressing the complex social, economic, and environmental challenges facing the world today.

Furthermore, ethical excellence in education helps to create a positive and productive learning environment. When students feel that they are treated fairly and with respect, they are more likely to be engaged and motivated in their learning. A positive learning environment also promotes a sense of belonging and community, which are essential for students' social and emotional development. In such an environment, students are more likely to collaborate, support one another, and work towards common goals.

Ethical excellence in education also plays a crucial role in fostering critical thinking and ethical decision-making skills. By engaging students in discussions and activities that explore ethical dilemmas and challenges, educators help to develop their ability to think critically, consider different perspectives, and make informed, ethical decisions. These skills are essential for success in the modern world, where individuals are constantly faced with complex and often conflicting choices.

The promotion of ethical excellence in education is a collective responsibility that involves educators, students, parents, and the wider community. It requires a commitment to continuous reflection and improvement, as well as the courage to address ethical challenges and stand up for what is right. By working together, we can create an educational system that not only imparts knowledge but also nurtures the ethical and moral development of future generations.

In conclusion, the importance of ethical excellence in education cannot be overstated. It is the foundation upon which a just and harmonious society is built. Ethical excellence involves a commitment to integrity, honesty, fairness, respect, responsibility, compassion, and empathy. It requires educators to lead by example, fostering a culture of trust, accountability, and ethical behavior. The impact of ethical excellence in education extends far beyond the classroom, shaping the character and actions of individuals and contributing to the greater good of society. By prioritizing ethical excellence in education, we can help to create a better, more just, and compassionate world for future generations.

ၦၦၦ

"Ethical excellence in education is not a destination but a continuous journey. It requires ongoing reflection and growth. Together, we build a foundation of integrity and compassion."

❦❦❦

TWO

FOUNDATIONS OF ETHICAL TEACHING: CORE PRINCIPLES AND VALUES

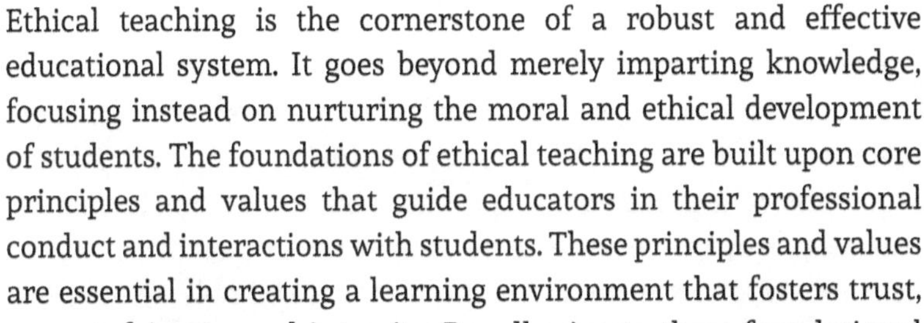

Ethical teaching is the cornerstone of a robust and effective educational system. It goes beyond merely imparting knowledge, focusing instead on nurturing the moral and ethical development of students. The foundations of ethical teaching are built upon core principles and values that guide educators in their professional conduct and interactions with students. These principles and values are essential in creating a learning environment that fosters trust, respect, fairness, and integrity. By adhering to these foundational elements, educators can inspire students to develop into responsible, ethical individuals who contribute positively to society.

One of the fundamental principles of ethical teaching is integrity. Integrity involves being honest, trustworthy, and transparent in all professional activities. For educators, this means being truthful in their communications, fair in their assessments, and consistent in their actions. Integrity is crucial because it builds trust between teachers and students, as well as among colleagues and the broader community. When educators demonstrate integrity, they set a powerful example for their students, encouraging them to adopt similar values in their own lives. Integrity also involves maintaining professional boundaries and avoiding conflicts of interest, ensuring that all interactions are conducted with the highest ethical standards.

Honesty is closely related to integrity and is another key component of ethical teaching. It requires educators to be truthful in their dealings with students, parents, and colleagues. This includes being honest about students' performance, providing constructive feedback, and acknowledging mistakes when they occur. Honesty fosters an environment of trust and respect, where students feel safe to express their thoughts and concerns. It also promotes academic integrity, as students are encouraged to produce original work and give proper credit to the sources they use. By modeling honesty, educators help students understand the importance of truthfulness in both their academic and personal lives.

Fairness is a critical value in ethical teaching, ensuring that all students are treated equitably and without bias. This principle involves providing equal opportunities for learning and growth, regardless of a student's background, abilities, or circumstances. Fairness requires educators to be aware of their own biases and to actively work to overcome them. It also means implementing fair assessment practices that accurately reflect each student's abilities and achievements. By being fair, educators create an inclusive environment where every student feels valued and respected. Fairness also extends to disciplinary actions, which should be applied consistently and without favoritism.

Respect is another foundational value in ethical teaching. It involves recognizing and honoring the inherent dignity and worth of every individual. For educators, this means treating students with kindness, listening to their concerns, and valuing their contributions. Respect also involves creating a classroom environment where diversity is celebrated, and differences are viewed as strengths. When educators demonstrate respect, they foster a positive and supportive learning environment where students feel safe and motivated to succeed. Respectful interactions also encourage students to treat others with kindness and consideration, promoting a culture of mutual respect within the school community.

Responsibility is a core principle that underpins ethical teaching. Educators have a responsibility to their students, their profession, and society as a whole. This responsibility includes providing high-quality education, fostering a love of learning, and preparing students to become responsible, engaged citizens. It also involves maintaining professional standards, engaging in continuous professional development, and contributing to the advancement of the educational field. Educators must take responsibility for their actions and decisions, ensuring that they act in the best interests of their students. By modeling responsibility, educators encourage students to take ownership of their own learning and to act responsibly in their interactions with others.

Compassion and empathy are essential components of ethical teaching, involving understanding and responding to the needs and challenges of others. Compassion requires educators to be sensitive to the emotional and social well-being of their students, offering support and encouragement when needed. Empathy involves putting oneself in another's shoes and experiencing their feelings and perspectives. By showing compassion and empathy, educators create a nurturing environment where students feel understood and cared for. These qualities are particularly important in addressing the diverse needs of students, including those who may be struggling academically, socially, or emotionally. Compassionate and empathetic educators build strong, positive relationships with their students, which are essential for effective teaching and learning.

Accountability is another key principle in ethical teaching, involving holding oneself and others responsible for their actions. Accountability means being answerable for the fairness and accuracy of assessments, the effectiveness of teaching methods, and the overall well-being of students. It also involves addressing ethical breaches promptly and fairly, whether they involve academic dishonesty, discrimination, or other forms of misconduct. By fostering a culture of accountability, educators help to maintain the integrity and credibility of the educational system. Accountability also includes reflecting on one's practice, seeking feedback, and making necessary improvements to enhance the quality of education.

Ethical teaching also requires a commitment to lifelong learning and professional growth. Educators must continuously seek to improve their knowledge and skills to provide the best possible education for their students. This commitment to professional development ensures that educators remain current with the latest research, teaching methods, and educational technologies. It also involves engaging in reflective practice, where educators critically evaluate their own teaching and seek ways to enhance their effectiveness. By valuing lifelong learning, educators model the importance of continuous growth and improvement for their students.

Ethical decision-making is a crucial aspect of ethical teaching, involving the ability to make informed and principled choices in complex situations. Educators often face ethical dilemmas where there may be conflicting interests or values. Ethical decision-making requires a careful consideration of all relevant factors, including the potential impact on students, colleagues, and the broader community. It involves seeking input from others, weighing the pros and cons, and making decisions that align with core ethical principles and values. Educators must also be prepared to justify their decisions and take responsibility for the outcomes. By practicing ethical decision-making, educators demonstrate integrity and fairness, setting a positive example for their students.

Creating a culture of ethical excellence in education involves fostering a collaborative and supportive environment where ethical behavior is encouraged and celebrated. This culture is built on open communication, mutual respect, and shared values. Educators, students, parents, and the wider community must work together to promote ethical principles and values. This collaborative approach helps to create a cohesive and inclusive learning environment where everyone feels valued and supported. Celebrating ethical behavior, such as recognizing acts of kindness, fairness, and integrity, reinforces the importance of these values and encourages others to follow suit.

The impact of ethical teaching extends far beyond the classroom, influencing students' behavior and attitudes in all areas of their lives. When students are taught and guided by ethically exemplary educators, they are more likely to develop into principled, responsible adults who contribute positively to society. Ethical education helps to cultivate a sense of moral responsibility, encouraging students to consider the impact of their actions on others and to strive for the greater good. This sense of moral responsibility is essential in addressing the complex social, economic, and environmental challenges facing the world today.

Moreover, ethical teaching enhances the overall quality of education by creating a positive and productive learning environment. When students feel that they are treated fairly and with respect, they are more likely to be engaged and motivated in their learning. A positive learning environment also promotes a sense of belonging and community, which are essential for students' social and emotional development. In such an environment, students are more likely to collaborate, support one another, and work towards common goals.

Ethical teaching also plays a crucial role in fostering critical thinking and ethical decision-making skills. By engaging students in discussions and activities that explore ethical dilemmas and challenges, educators help to develop their ability to think critically, consider different perspectives, and make informed, ethical decisions. These skills are essential for success in the modern world, where individuals are constantly faced with complex and often conflicting choices.

In addition to benefiting students, ethical teaching also has positive implications for educators and the broader educational community. Educators who adhere to ethical principles and values are more likely to experience job satisfaction, professional fulfillment, and a sense of purpose in their work. Ethical teaching also enhances the reputation and credibility of the educational institution, fostering trust and confidence among students, parents, and the wider community. This trust is essential for building strong partnerships and collaborations that support the overall mission of the educational institution.

The promotion of ethical teaching is a collective responsibility that involves educators, students, parents, and the wider community. It requires a commitment to continuous reflection and improvement, as well as the courage to address ethical challenges and stand up for what is right. By working together, we can create an educational system that not only imparts knowledge but also nurtures the ethical and moral development of future generations.

The foundations of ethical teaching are built upon core principles and values that guide educators in their professional conduct and interactions with students. These principles and values, including integrity, honesty, fairness, respect, responsibility, compassion, empathy, and accountability, are essential in creating a positive and productive learning environment. Ethical teaching involves a commitment to lifelong learning, professional growth, and ethical decision-making. It also requires fostering a culture of ethical excellence through collaboration, open communication, and mutual respect. The impact of ethical teaching extends far beyond the classroom, shaping the character and actions of individuals and contributing to the greater good of society. By prioritizing ethical teaching, we can help to create a better, more just, and compassionate world for future generations.

ϼϼϼ

"Educators are more than conveyors of knowledge; they are role models of ethical behavior. Their actions shape the values of future generations. Every decision they make impacts the moral compass of their students."

THREE

THE ROLE OF INTEGRITY IN THE CLASSROOM

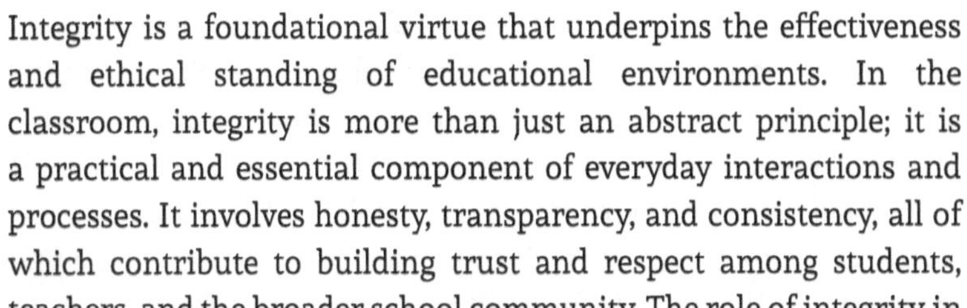

Integrity is a foundational virtue that underpins the effectiveness and ethical standing of educational environments. In the classroom, integrity is more than just an abstract principle; it is a practical and essential component of everyday interactions and processes. It involves honesty, transparency, and consistency, all of which contribute to building trust and respect among students, teachers, and the broader school community. The role of integrity in the classroom extends beyond individual behavior to influence the overall culture and success of the educational system.

Integrity in the classroom starts with the educator. Teachers serve as role models, and their actions significantly impact students' attitudes and behaviors. When teachers demonstrate integrity, they set a powerful example for students to follow. This demonstration includes being honest in communication, fair in assessments, and consistent in enforcing rules and expectations. By embodying integrity, teachers foster an environment where students feel safe, respected, and motivated to learn. This environment is crucial for effective teaching and learning, as it allows students to focus on their studies without fear of bias or unfair treatment.

Honesty is a key aspect of integrity. In the classroom, honesty manifests in various ways, such as providing truthful feedback, acknowledging mistakes, and being transparent about expectations and grading criteria. When teachers are honest, they build trust with their students. Trust, in turn, enhances student engagement and participation. Students are more likely to take risks, ask questions, and seek help when they know that their teacher is reliable and truthful. Moreover, honesty in assessment practices ensures that students receive accurate and fair evaluations of their performance, which is essential for their academic growth and development.

Transparency is closely related to honesty and is another vital component of integrity in the classroom. Transparency involves clear and open communication about classroom policies, procedures, and expectations. It means that students understand what is required of them and what they can expect from their teacher. When teachers are transparent, they create a predictable and stable learning environment. This stability helps students feel secure and supported, which is important for their emotional and academic well-being. Additionally, transparency helps prevent misunderstandings and conflicts, as everyone is aware of the rules and procedures that govern the classroom.

Consistency is another important aspect of integrity. Consistency involves applying rules and expectations fairly and uniformly to all students. It means that all students are held to the same standards and that disciplinary actions are administered impartially. When teachers are consistent, they establish a sense of fairness and equity in the classroom. Students are more likely to respect and follow rules when they know that they are applied consistently and without favoritism. Consistency also helps to build a positive classroom culture where students understand the consequences of their actions and are motivated to behave ethically.

Building trust is one of the most significant roles of integrity in the classroom. Trust is the foundation of positive relationships between teachers and students. When students trust their teacher, they are more likely to be engaged, motivated, and willing to take academic risks. Trust also encourages open communication, allowing students to express their thoughts, concerns, and questions without fear of judgment or retribution. This open communication is essential for effective teaching and learning, as it enables teachers to understand and address students' needs and challenges. Furthermore, trust fosters a sense of belonging and community in the classroom, which is important for students' social and emotional development.

Integrity also plays a crucial role in fostering a positive classroom culture. A classroom culture rooted in integrity is characterized by mutual respect, fairness, and ethical behavior. In such a culture, students feel valued and respected, which enhances their self-esteem and motivation to learn. Moreover, a positive classroom culture promotes collaboration and cooperation among students. When students see their teacher acting with integrity, they are more likely to emulate these behaviors in their interactions with peers. This emulation creates a supportive and inclusive learning environment where students work together to achieve common goals.

Integrity in the classroom also has a significant impact on academic integrity. Academic integrity involves upholding ethical standards in all aspects of academic work, including assignments, assessments, and research. When teachers model integrity, they reinforce the importance of academic honesty and discourage cheating, plagiarism, and other forms of academic misconduct. Teachers can promote academic integrity by setting clear expectations, providing guidance on proper citation practices, and fostering a culture of honesty and responsibility. Additionally, teachers can implement strategies to prevent and address academic misconduct, such as using plagiarism detection tools and designing assessments that encourage original thinking and creativity.

The role of integrity in the classroom extends to the relationships between teachers and parents. Honest and transparent communication with parents is essential for building trust and collaboration. When teachers communicate openly and honestly with parents, they create a partnership that supports students' academic and personal development. This partnership is important for addressing students' needs and challenges, as well as for celebrating their successes. By maintaining integrity in their interactions with parents, teachers demonstrate their commitment to the well-being and success of their students.

Integrity also plays a critical role in professional conduct and collaboration among educators. Teachers who act with integrity contribute to a positive and supportive school culture. They collaborate with colleagues, share best practices, and support one another in their professional growth and development. Integrity in professional conduct involves being honest and transparent in communications, respecting colleagues' contributions, and upholding ethical standards in all professional activities. By fostering a culture of integrity, schools create an environment where educators feel valued, respected, and motivated to excel in their teaching.

The impact of integrity in the classroom extends beyond the immediate school environment to influence the broader community. When students learn the importance of integrity and ethical behavior, they carry these values with them into their future endeavors. They become responsible and ethical citizens who contribute positively to society. Moreover, a commitment to integrity in education helps to build public trust and confidence in the educational system. Communities are more likely to support and invest in schools when they see that educators are dedicated to upholding high ethical standards.

Integrity in the classroom also plays a crucial role in addressing ethical dilemmas and challenges. Teachers often face complex situations where there may be conflicting interests or values. Integrity involves making ethical decisions that prioritize the well-being and best interests of students. It requires a careful consideration of all relevant factors, including the potential impact on students, colleagues, and the broader community. By adhering to ethical principles and values, teachers can navigate these challenges and make decisions that uphold the integrity of the educational system.

Reflective practice is an important aspect of maintaining integrity in the classroom. Reflective practice involves regularly evaluating one's actions, decisions, and interactions to ensure that they align with ethical principles and values. Teachers can engage in reflective practice by seeking feedback from students, colleagues, and parents, and by critically examining their own teaching practices. This reflection helps educators to identify areas for improvement and to make necessary changes to enhance their effectiveness and ethical conduct. By prioritizing reflective practice, teachers demonstrate their commitment to continuous growth and professional development.

Professional development is also essential for maintaining and enhancing integrity in the classroom. Ongoing professional development helps educators to stay current with the latest research, teaching methods, and ethical standards. It provides opportunities for teachers to learn new strategies for promoting integrity and ethical behavior in the classroom. Additionally, professional development fosters a culture of lifelong learning and continuous improvement, which are important aspects of integrity. By investing in their own professional growth, teachers show their dedication to providing the best possible education for their students.

The role of integrity in the classroom is multifaceted and far-reaching. Integrity involves honesty, transparency, and consistency, all of which contribute to building trust and respect among students, teachers, and the broader school community. It sets the foundation for positive relationships, a supportive classroom culture, and academic integrity. By embodying integrity, teachers create an environment where students feel valued, respected, and motivated to learn. The impact of integrity extends beyond the classroom, influencing students' behavior and attitudes in all areas of their lives and contributing to the greater good of society. Moreover, integrity in professional conduct and collaboration among educators enhances the overall effectiveness and ethical standing of the educational system. By prioritizing integrity, educators can inspire students to develop into responsible, ethical individuals who contribute positively to society.

᠔᠔᠔

"Embedding ethics in the curriculum transforms learning into a holistic experience. It teaches students to think critically about moral issues. This prepares them for the complex ethical landscapes of adulthood."

❥❥❥

FOUR

Promoting Honesty Among Students and Educators

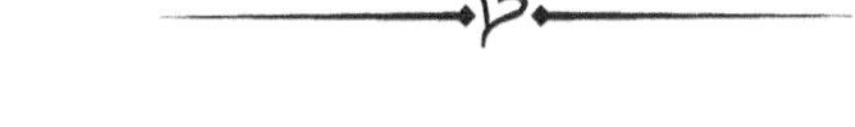

Promoting honesty among students and educators is fundamental to fostering a culture of trust, integrity, and academic excellence within educational environments. Honesty is a cornerstone of ethical behavior, and its promotion is essential for creating a learning atmosphere where students feel safe, respected, and motivated to engage in their studies. For educators, modeling honesty sets a standard for professional conduct that influences their interactions with students, colleagues, and the broader school community. Cultivating honesty requires a multifaceted approach that includes clear communication, ethical leadership, supportive policies, and a commitment to creating an environment where truthfulness is valued and upheld.

Honesty in education begins with the establishment of clear expectations and guidelines. Educators must communicate the importance of honesty in all aspects of academic work, including assignments, assessments, and classroom interactions. This communication should outline what constitutes honest behavior and the consequences of dishonest actions such as cheating, plagiarism, and falsifying information. By setting clear expectations, educators provide students with a framework for understanding the value of honesty and the impact of their actions on their learning and the integrity of the educational institution.

Modeling honest behavior is one of the most effective ways educators can promote honesty among students. Teachers who consistently demonstrate honesty in their actions and communications serve as role models for their students. This modeling includes being truthful in feedback, admitting mistakes, and being transparent about classroom policies and grading criteria. When students see their teachers valuing honesty and acting with integrity, they are more likely to emulate these behaviors in their own academic and personal lives. This modeling also helps to build a trusting relationship between students and teachers, which is crucial for fostering an environment where students feel comfortable being honest.

Creating a supportive and inclusive classroom environment is essential for promoting honesty. Students are more likely to be truthful when they feel respected, valued, and understood. Educators can foster this environment by encouraging open communication, actively listening to students' concerns, and providing a safe space for students to express themselves without fear of judgment or retribution. When students know that their voices are heard and their perspectives are considered, they are more likely to engage honestly in their academic work and interactions.

Another key aspect of promoting honesty is the implementation of fair and transparent assessment practices. Assessments should be designed to accurately measure students' knowledge and skills without encouraging dishonest behavior. This involves creating assignments and tests that are clear, relevant, and appropriately challenging. Additionally, educators should provide guidance on how to properly cite sources and avoid plagiarism. By teaching students the skills needed to complete their work honestly, educators help to reduce the temptation to engage in dishonest practices.

The use of formative assessments can also support honesty by emphasizing learning and improvement over grades. Formative assessments provide ongoing feedback that helps students identify their strengths and areas for growth. This approach reduces the pressure to perform perfectly on summative assessments and encourages students to focus on their learning journey. When students understand that mistakes are part of the learning process and that they will not be penalized for being honest about their struggles, they are more likely to engage authentically with their work.

Addressing incidents of dishonesty promptly and fairly is crucial for maintaining an environment of trust and integrity. When dishonest behavior is detected, educators must respond consistently and transparently, ensuring that students understand the consequences of their actions. This response should be guided by the principles of fairness and respect, aiming to educate rather than simply punish. For example, if a student is caught plagiarizing, the educator might provide an opportunity for the student to redo the assignment with proper citations and offer additional support to help the student understand the importance of academic integrity. By addressing dishonesty in a constructive manner, educators reinforce the value of honesty and help students learn from their mistakes.

Fostering a school-wide culture that prioritizes honesty requires collaboration among all members of the educational community, including administrators, teachers, students, and parents. School policies and practices should reflect a commitment to honesty and integrity. This includes having clear codes of conduct, honor codes, and academic integrity policies that are communicated to all stakeholders. Schools can also provide professional development opportunities for educators to learn strategies for promoting honesty and addressing dishonesty effectively. By working together, the school community can create a cohesive and supportive environment that values and upholds honest behavior.

Encouraging student leadership and involvement in promoting honesty can also be highly effective. Student-led initiatives, such as honor councils or peer mentoring programs, can empower students to take an active role in fostering a culture of honesty. These initiatives provide opportunities for students to discuss the importance of honesty, share strategies for maintaining academic integrity, and support their peers in making ethical decisions. When students take ownership of promoting honesty, they help to create a peer culture that values truthfulness and integrity.

Recognizing and celebrating honest behavior is another important strategy for promoting honesty. Schools can implement recognition programs that highlight students and educators who exemplify honesty in their actions and interactions. This recognition can take many forms, such as awards, certificates, or public acknowledgments during school assemblies. Celebrating honest behavior reinforces its importance and encourages others to follow suit. Additionally, recognition programs can help to build a positive school culture where ethical behavior is valued and rewarded.

Incorporating discussions about honesty and ethical behavior into the curriculum can further support the promotion of honesty. Educators can integrate lessons on ethics, moral decision-making, and the consequences of dishonest behavior into various subjects. For example, in language arts classes, students might analyze characters' decisions and actions in literature, while in social studies, they might explore historical events through the lens of ethical considerations. By embedding these discussions into the curriculum, educators help students to develop a deeper understanding of the importance of honesty and the complexities of ethical decision-making.

Providing students with opportunities to practice honesty in real-world situations is also beneficial. Service-learning projects, internships, and other experiential learning opportunities allow students to apply their ethical principles in practical settings. These experiences help students to see the real-world implications of honesty and to develop a strong commitment to ethical behavior. Additionally, reflecting on these experiences through discussions and written reflections can help students to internalize the value of honesty and to understand how it applies to their personal and professional lives.

The role of technology in promoting honesty is increasingly important in today's digital age. Schools must address the challenges and opportunities that technology presents in relation to academic integrity. This includes teaching students about the ethical use of digital resources, the importance of proper citation, and the risks of plagiarism and cheating in online environments. Schools can also use technology to support honest behavior, such as implementing plagiarism detection software and using online platforms that promote transparency in assessments and feedback. By leveraging technology thoughtfully, educators can help students to navigate the digital landscape with integrity.

Building strong relationships between educators and students is fundamental to promoting honesty. When students feel connected to their teachers and believe that their teachers care about their well-being, they are more likely to act honestly. Educators can build these relationships by showing genuine interest in students' lives, providing individualized support, and creating a classroom environment where every student feels valued. Strong relationships foster trust, which is essential for encouraging honest behavior.

Parental involvement is also critical in promoting honesty among students. Schools should engage parents in discussions about the importance of honesty and provide them with resources to support their children in developing ethical behavior. By involving parents in the process, schools can create a unified approach to promoting honesty that extends beyond the classroom. Parents can reinforce the values of honesty at home and support their children in understanding the importance of ethical behavior.

Continuous reflection and improvement are necessary for sustaining a culture of honesty in education. Schools should regularly evaluate their policies, practices, and strategies for promoting honesty to ensure that they are effective and relevant. This evaluation can involve gathering feedback from students, educators, and parents, as well as reviewing incidents of dishonesty to identify patterns and areas for improvement. By committing to ongoing reflection and improvement, schools demonstrate their dedication to fostering an environment where honesty is valued and upheld.

Promoting honesty among students and educators is essential for creating a culture of trust, integrity, and academic excellence. This promotion requires a multifaceted approach that includes clear communication, ethical leadership, supportive policies, and a commitment to creating an environment where truthfulness is valued and upheld. Educators play a crucial role in modeling honest behavior and setting clear expectations for academic integrity. Creating a supportive and inclusive classroom environment, implementing fair and transparent assessment practices, and addressing incidents of dishonesty promptly and fairly are all important strategies for promoting honesty.

Collaboration among all members of the school community, including students, educators, parents, and administrators, is necessary for fostering a cohesive and supportive environment that prioritizes honesty. Recognizing and celebrating honest behavior, incorporating discussions about ethics into the curriculum, and providing opportunities for real-world practice further support the promotion of honesty. By committing to continuous reflection and improvement, schools can sustain a culture of honesty that prepares students to become responsible, ethical individuals who contribute positively to society.

ϷϷϷ

"Creating an inclusive school environment is
fundamental to fostering ethical behavior. When
students feel valued and respected, they thrive.
Inclusivity and fairness pave the way for mutual
respect and understanding."

ᐅᐅᐅ

FIVE

COMPASSION AND EMPATHY: BUILDING A CARING EDUCATIONAL ENVIRONMENT

Compassion and empathy are fundamental to creating a caring and supportive educational environment. These qualities not only enhance the well-being of students but also foster an atmosphere where learning can thrive. Compassion involves recognizing and alleviating the suffering of others, while empathy involves understanding and sharing the feelings of another person. When educators practice compassion and empathy, they build trust, encourage open communication, and create a sense of belonging that is essential for both academic and personal growth. Building a caring educational environment requires a commitment to these values at all levels of the educational system, from individual interactions in the classroom to school-wide policies and practices.

At the heart of a compassionate and empathetic educational environment is the relationship between educators and students. Teachers who demonstrate compassion and empathy create a safe space where students feel valued and understood. This sense of safety is crucial for students to take academic risks, ask questions, and express their thoughts and feelings without fear of judgment. When students perceive their teachers as caring and empathetic, they are more likely to engage actively in their learning and to develop positive attitudes towards school. These positive relationships also provide a strong foundation for addressing the diverse needs of students, including those who may be struggling academically, socially, or emotionally.

Compassion and empathy in education begin with active listening. Active listening involves fully focusing on the speaker, understanding their message, and responding thoughtfully. When teachers practice active listening, they show students that their voices matter and that their experiences and perspectives are important. This validation can significantly impact a student's self-esteem and motivation. Additionally, active listening helps educators to identify and address the specific needs and concerns of their students. By being attentive and responsive, teachers can provide appropriate support and interventions that enhance student learning and well-being.

Another critical aspect of building a compassionate and empathetic educational environment is creating an inclusive classroom culture. An inclusive classroom recognizes and celebrates the diversity of students, including differences in background, ability, and experience. Teachers can foster inclusivity by incorporating diverse perspectives into the curriculum, using culturally responsive teaching practices, and creating opportunities for all students to participate and contribute. An inclusive environment not only promotes equity and respect but also helps students to develop empathy by exposing them to different viewpoints and experiences.

When students learn to appreciate and understand diversity, they are better equipped to empathize with others and to act compassionately in their interactions.

Modeling compassionate and empathetic behavior is one of the most effective ways educators can instill these values in their students. Teachers who consistently demonstrate kindness, understanding, and support set a powerful example for their students to follow. This modeling can occur in everyday interactions, such as offering a listening ear to a student in distress, providing encouragement and positive feedback, or showing patience and understanding when students make mistakes. By embodying compassion and empathy, educators create a ripple effect that influences the behavior and attitudes of their students. Over time, students learn to internalize these values and to apply them in their own interactions with peers and others.

Creating opportunities for students to practice compassion and empathy is also essential for building a caring educational environment. Service-learning projects, peer mentoring programs, and collaborative activities provide students with hands-on experiences in which they can develop and demonstrate these qualities. Service-learning projects, for example, allow students to engage with their communities and to make a positive impact through acts of service. These projects help students to see the real-world implications of compassion and empathy and to understand the importance of giving back to others. Peer mentoring programs, where older students support and guide younger students, also foster a sense of responsibility and empathy. Through these experiences, students learn to recognize the needs of others and to take action to support and uplift their peers.

Empathy can also be cultivated through curriculum and instruction. Integrating social-emotional learning (SEL) into the curriculum provides students with the tools and skills needed to develop empathy and compassion. SEL programs focus on teaching students to recognize and manage their emotions, to develop positive relationships, and to make responsible decisions. By incorporating SEL into everyday instruction, educators help students to build the emotional intelligence necessary for empathetic and compassionate behavior. Literature, history, and the arts are particularly effective subjects for exploring empathy, as they often involve the study of human experiences and emotions. By engaging with stories and historical events, students can develop a deeper understanding of the perspectives and feelings of others.

Creating a supportive school culture that prioritizes the well-being of all members of the school community is crucial for fostering compassion and empathy. School leaders play a key role in setting the tone for this culture by promoting policies and practices that support emotional and social well-being. This includes providing professional development opportunities for educators to learn about compassionate and empathetic teaching practices, as well as implementing programs that support the mental health and well-being of students and staff. A supportive school culture also involves recognizing and celebrating acts of kindness and empathy, creating a positive and reinforcing environment where these values are valued and upheld.

In addition to supporting students, it is important to recognize the role of compassion and empathy in relationships among educators and staff. A caring and supportive work environment enhances collaboration, reduces stress, and promotes job satisfaction. When educators feel supported and understood by their colleagues and administrators, they are better equipped to provide compassionate and empathetic support to their students. School leaders can foster a supportive work environment by promoting open communication, providing opportunities for professional collaboration, and recognizing the contributions of all staff members. By creating a culture of care and support among educators, schools can ensure that these values permeate all aspects of the educational environment.

Parental and community involvement is another important factor in building a caring educational environment. Engaging parents and community members in the educational process helps to create a network of support for students and reinforces the values of compassion and empathy. Schools can involve parents by providing opportunities for them to participate in school activities, by offering resources and workshops on supporting their children's emotional and social development, and by fostering open lines of communication. Community partnerships, such as collaborations with local organizations and businesses, can also provide additional resources and support for students and families. By working together, schools, parents, and community members can create a comprehensive and supportive environment that promotes the well-being and success of all students.

It is also important to consider the impact of technology on the cultivation of compassion and empathy in education. While technology offers many benefits for learning and communication, it also presents challenges, such as the potential for cyberbullying and social isolation. Educators can address these challenges by teaching students about digital citizenship and the responsible use of technology. This includes educating students about the impact of their online behavior on others and encouraging them to use technology in ways that promote positive and respectful interactions. Additionally, technology can be used to enhance empathy by connecting students with diverse perspectives and experiences through virtual exchanges, online collaborations, and digital storytelling. By integrating technology thoughtfully, educators can leverage its potential to support the development of compassion and empathy in students.

Continuous reflection and improvement are essential for sustaining a caring educational environment. Schools should regularly evaluate their policies, practices, and strategies for promoting compassion and empathy to ensure that they are effective and relevant. This evaluation can involve gathering feedback from students, educators, parents, and community members, as well as reviewing data on student well-being and academic outcomes. By committing to ongoing reflection and improvement, schools demonstrate their dedication to fostering an environment where compassion and empathy are prioritized and upheld.

Building a caring educational environment through compassion and empathy is fundamental to the success and well-being of students and educators. Compassion involves recognizing and alleviating the suffering of others, while empathy involves understanding and sharing the feelings of another person. These qualities are essential for creating a learning atmosphere where students feel safe, valued, and motivated to engage in their studies. Educators play a crucial role in modeling compassionate and empathetic behavior, setting clear expectations, and creating opportunities for students to practice these values.

By fostering an inclusive classroom culture, integrating social-emotional learning into the curriculum, and creating a supportive school culture, educators can build a caring educational environment that supports the academic and personal growth of all students. Collaboration among educators, parents, and community members is also important for creating a comprehensive network of support. By committing to continuous reflection and improvement, schools can sustain an environment where compassion and empathy are prioritized and upheld, preparing students to become responsible, ethical individuals who contribute positively to society.

ᕈᕈᕈ

"The role of ethical leadership in education cannot be overstated. Leaders set the tone for the entire school community. Their commitment to transparency and accountability inspires others to uphold the same values."

❤❤❤

SIX

RESPECT AND RESPONSIBILITY: KEY PILLARS OF ETHICAL CONDUCT

Respect and responsibility are key pillars of ethical conduct, essential for the functioning of any educational environment. These values form the foundation of positive relationships, effective teaching and learning, and a cohesive school culture. Respect involves recognizing and valuing the inherent worth of each individual, treating them with dignity and consideration. Responsibility involves being accountable for one's actions, fulfilling one's duties, and contributing positively to the community. Together, respect and responsibility create a framework that supports ethical behavior and fosters a positive, inclusive, and productive educational setting.

Respect in education begins with the recognition of the intrinsic worth of every individual, including students, teachers, staff, and administrators. This recognition involves treating everyone with kindness, fairness, and dignity, regardless of their background, abilities, or beliefs. Respectful behavior sets the tone for all interactions within the school, promoting a culture of mutual consideration and understanding. When students and educators feel respected, they are more likely to engage positively in the learning process and to contribute to a supportive and collaborative school environment.

One of the most important ways to demonstrate respect in the classroom is through active listening. Active listening involves paying full attention to the speaker, understanding their message, and responding thoughtfully. For educators, this means genuinely listening to students' questions, concerns, and ideas without interrupting or dismissing them. When teachers practice active listening, they show students that their voices are valued and that their contributions are important. This validation fosters a sense of belonging and encourages students to participate actively in their education. Additionally, active listening helps to build trust between teachers and students, which is crucial for creating a safe and supportive learning environment.

Respect also involves creating an inclusive classroom where diversity is celebrated and differences are viewed as strengths. An inclusive classroom recognizes the unique contributions of each student and provides equal opportunities for all to succeed. Educators can foster inclusivity by incorporating diverse perspectives into the curriculum, using culturally responsive teaching practices, and creating opportunities for all students to participate and contribute. When students see their identities and experiences reflected and valued in the classroom, they are more likely to feel respected and engaged in their learning. Inclusivity also promotes empathy and understanding, helping students to appreciate and respect the diverse backgrounds and viewpoints of their peers.

In addition to fostering respect among students, educators must also demonstrate respect for their colleagues and the broader school community. This involves treating all staff members with kindness, fairness, and professionalism. Respectful interactions among educators create a positive work environment that supports collaboration and professional growth. When teachers respect one another, they are more likely to share ideas, support each other's efforts, and work together to enhance the educational experience for their students. This collaborative culture benefits everyone in the school community and contributes to a cohesive and effective educational system.

Responsibility is another key pillar of ethical conduct, involving accountability and the fulfillment of one's duties. For students, responsibility means taking ownership of their learning, completing assignments on time, and adhering to school rules and expectations. It also involves being accountable for their actions and understanding the impact of their behavior on others. Educators play a crucial role in teaching students about responsibility by setting clear expectations, providing guidance and support, and modeling responsible behavior. When students learn to take responsibility for their actions, they develop important life skills that will serve them well in their academic and personal lives.

Educators themselves must also demonstrate responsibility in their professional conduct. This includes being prepared for classes, providing high-quality instruction, and continuously seeking to improve their teaching practices. It also involves being accountable for the fairness and accuracy of assessments, the effectiveness of teaching methods, and the overall well-being of students. By fulfilling their professional responsibilities, educators set a positive example for their students and contribute to a culture of accountability within the school. Additionally, responsible behavior by educators helps to build trust with students, parents, and colleagues, which is essential for creating a supportive and effective educational environment.

Responsibility also extends to the broader community, as schools have a duty to contribute positively to society. This involves preparing students to be responsible, engaged citizens who can make meaningful contributions to their communities. Schools can promote this sense of civic responsibility by incorporating community service projects, civic education, and opportunities for student leadership into the curriculum. These activities help students to understand their role in society and to develop the skills and values necessary to be responsible and active participants in their communities. By fostering a sense of responsibility in students, schools help to create a generation of ethical and engaged citizens who can address the challenges of the future.

Creating a culture of respect and responsibility requires a collaborative effort from all members of the school community. School leaders play a key role in setting the tone for this culture by promoting policies and practices that support respectful and responsible behavior. This includes implementing codes of conduct, providing professional development opportunities for educators, and recognizing and celebrating acts of respect and responsibility. By prioritizing these values, school leaders can create an environment where ethical behavior is valued and upheld.

Parents and community members also play an important role in promoting respect and responsibility. Engaging parents in the educational process helps to reinforce these values at home and in the community. Schools can involve parents by providing opportunities for them to participate in school activities, offering resources and workshops on supporting their children's development, and fostering open lines of communication. Community partnerships, such as collaborations with local organizations and businesses, can also provide additional resources and support for promoting respect and responsibility. By working together, schools, parents, and community members can create a comprehensive network of support that fosters ethical behavior and positive contributions to society.

It is also important to recognize the role of respect and responsibility in addressing ethical dilemmas and challenges within the school community. Educators often face complex situations where there may be conflicting interests or values. In such cases, respect and responsibility can guide ethical decision-making by ensuring that all perspectives are considered and that actions are taken with integrity and accountability. This involves being transparent about the decision-making process, seeking input from others, and making decisions that prioritize the well-being and best interests of students. By adhering to the principles of respect and responsibility, educators can navigate these challenges in a way that upholds ethical standards and fosters trust within the school community.

Continuous reflection and improvement are essential for sustaining a culture of respect and responsibility. Schools should regularly evaluate their policies, practices, and strategies for promoting these values to ensure that they are effective and relevant. This evaluation can involve gathering feedback from students, educators, parents, and community members, as well as reviewing data on student behavior and academic outcomes. By committing to ongoing reflection and improvement, schools demonstrate their dedication to fostering an environment where respect and responsibility are prioritized and upheld.

Respect and responsibility are key pillars of ethical conduct that are essential for creating a positive, inclusive, and productive educational environment. Respect involves recognizing and valuing the inherent worth of each individual, treating them with dignity and consideration. Responsibility involves being accountable for one's actions, fulfilling one's duties, and contributing positively to the community. Together, these values form the foundation of positive relationships, effective teaching and learning, and a cohesive school culture.

Educators play a crucial role in modeling respectful and responsible behavior, setting clear expectations, and creating opportunities for students to develop these values. Collaboration among all members of the school community, including educators, students, parents, and community members, is necessary for fostering a comprehensive network of support. By committing to continuous reflection and improvement, schools can sustain an environment where respect and responsibility are prioritized and upheld, preparing students to become responsible, ethical individuals who contribute positively to society.

ᐅᐅᐅ

"Parents and community members are vital partners in ethical education. Their involvement reinforces the values taught in schools. Together, they create a cohesive support system for students."

ppp

SEVEN

FAIRNESS AND EQUITY: ENSURING JUSTICE IN EDUCATIONAL PRACTICES

Fairness and equity are fundamental principles that ensure justice in educational practices, forming the backbone of a just and inclusive educational environment. These principles demand that every student, regardless of their background, abilities, or circumstances, receives equal opportunities to succeed and thrive. In an educational context, fairness involves treating students impartially and providing them with the support they need to achieve their potential, while equity goes a step further by recognizing that different students may require different resources and accommodations to achieve similar outcomes. Ensuring fairness and equity in education is essential for fostering a learning environment where all students feel valued, respected, and capable of achieving their best.

At its core, fairness in education means creating conditions where every student has an equal chance to succeed. This involves implementing policies and practices that ensure impartial treatment and prevent discrimination based on race, gender, socioeconomic status, disability, or any other characteristic. Fairness requires that educators assess students' work and behavior using consistent and transparent criteria, providing equal access to learning resources and opportunities. When students perceive that they are being treated fairly, they are more likely to engage positively with their education, trust their teachers, and feel motivated to put forth their best effort.

Equity, on the other hand, recognizes that students come to the classroom with diverse needs, experiences, and challenges. Achieving equity involves identifying and addressing the specific barriers that different students face and providing the necessary resources and support to help them overcome these obstacles. This might include differentiated instruction, individualized learning plans, additional academic support, and accommodations for students with disabilities. By tailoring educational practices to meet the diverse needs of students, educators can help ensure that every student has the opportunity to succeed, regardless of their starting point.

One of the key aspects of promoting fairness and equity in education is addressing the achievement gap, which refers to the persistent disparities in academic performance between different groups of students, often along lines of race, ethnicity, socioeconomic status, and disability. To close the achievement gap, educators must implement targeted interventions and support systems that address the root causes of these disparities. This might involve providing extra tutoring, mentoring programs, access to advanced coursework, and other resources that help level the playing field for disadvantaged students. Additionally, schools must work to create a culturally responsive and inclusive curriculum that reflects the diverse experiences and perspectives of all students, helping to engage and motivate them to succeed.

Another important aspect of fairness and equity in education is the fair and unbiased assessment of student performance. Traditional assessment methods, such as standardized tests, can sometimes perpetuate inequities by failing to account for the diverse backgrounds and learning styles of students. To promote fairness, educators should employ a variety of assessment methods that provide a more comprehensive and accurate picture of students' abilities and progress. This might include formative assessments, performance-based assessments, and portfolios, which allow students to demonstrate their learning in different ways and provide multiple opportunities for success. Additionally, assessments should be designed and administered in a way that is accessible to all students, including those with disabilities or language barriers.

Creating an inclusive classroom environment is also crucial for promoting fairness and equity. An inclusive classroom values and respects the diversity of students and creates a sense of belonging for all. This involves using teaching strategies that are responsive to the diverse cultural, linguistic, and learning needs of students. Educators can promote inclusivity by incorporating diverse perspectives into the curriculum, using culturally responsive teaching practices, and fostering a classroom culture where all students feel valued and respected. Inclusive practices help to create a supportive learning environment where all students can thrive, regardless of their background or abilities.

Professional development for educators is essential for promoting fairness and equity in education. Teachers and school leaders need ongoing training and support to develop the knowledge, skills, and attitudes necessary to create equitable learning environments. This training should include topics such as cultural competence, implicit bias, differentiated instruction, and inclusive teaching practices. By providing educators with the tools and resources they need to address the diverse needs of their students, schools can help ensure that all students receive a fair and equitable education.

Parental and community involvement is another important factor in promoting fairness and equity in education. Engaging parents and community members in the educational process helps to create a network of support for students and reinforces the values of fairness and equity. Schools can involve parents by providing opportunities for them to participate in school activities, offering resources and workshops on supporting their children's development, and fostering open lines of communication. Community partnerships, such as collaborations with local organizations and businesses, can also provide additional resources and support for promoting fairness and equity. By working together, schools, parents, and community members can create a comprehensive and supportive environment that promotes the well-being and success of all students.

Addressing systemic inequities in education requires a commitment to continuous reflection and improvement. Schools should regularly evaluate their policies, practices, and strategies for promoting fairness and equity to ensure that they are effective and relevant. This evaluation can involve gathering feedback from students, educators, parents, and community members, as well as reviewing data on student performance and outcomes. By committing to ongoing reflection and improvement, schools can identify areas for growth and make necessary changes to better support all students.

One critical area of focus for promoting fairness and equity is the allocation of resources. Schools must ensure that resources are distributed in a way that addresses the needs of all students, particularly those who are disadvantaged or marginalized. This might involve providing additional funding for schools in low-income areas, ensuring that all students have access to high-quality instructional materials and technology, and providing targeted support services for students who need them. Equitable resource allocation helps to create a level playing field and ensures that all students have the tools and opportunities they need to succeed.

Creating policies that support fairness and equity is also essential. School policies should be designed to promote inclusive practices, prevent discrimination, and ensure that all students have access to the opportunities and support they need to succeed. This might include policies related to admissions, discipline, special education, and student support services. Policies should be regularly reviewed and updated to ensure that they are effective and aligned with the principles of fairness and equity. Additionally, schools should involve students, parents, and community members in the policy-making process to ensure that their perspectives and needs are taken into account.

Promoting fairness and equity also involves addressing the broader social and economic factors that impact students' education. Schools must work to create partnerships with community organizations, government agencies, and businesses to address issues such as poverty, housing instability, and health disparities that can affect students' ability to succeed in school. By addressing these broader issues, schools can help to create a more equitable and supportive environment for all students.

Another important aspect of promoting fairness and equity is fostering a school culture that values diversity and inclusion. This involves creating a positive and supportive environment where all students feel welcome and valued. Schools can promote a culture of inclusion by celebrating diversity, promoting positive relationships among students and staff, and addressing issues of bias and discrimination when they arise. A positive school culture helps to create a sense of belonging and ensures that all students feel supported and motivated to succeed.

Finally, promoting fairness and equity requires a commitment to advocacy and social justice. Educators, school leaders, and policymakers must be willing to advocate for policies and practices that promote equity and address systemic inequities in education. This might involve advocating for increased funding for schools in low-income areas, promoting policies that support inclusive practices, and working to address broader social and economic issues that impact students' education. By advocating for fairness and equity, educators and school leaders can help to create a more just and inclusive educational system that supports the success and well-being of all students.

Fairness and equity are essential principles for ensuring justice in educational practices. These principles require that every student, regardless of their background, abilities, or circumstances, receives equal opportunities to succeed. Fairness involves treating students impartially and providing them with the support they need to achieve their potential, while equity goes a step further by recognizing that different students may require different resources and accommodations to achieve similar outcomes. Promoting fairness and equity involves implementing policies and practices that ensure impartial treatment, addressing the diverse needs of students, and creating an inclusive and supportive learning environment. It also requires a commitment to continuous reflection and improvement, equitable resource allocation, inclusive policies, and advocacy for social justice. By prioritizing fairness and equity, schools can create a just and inclusive educational environment that supports the success and well-being of all students.

ᐅᐅᐅ

"In the digital age, teaching responsible use of technology is crucial. Students must understand the ethical implications of their online actions. Digital literacy and ethics go hand in hand."

ᗡᗡᗡ

EIGHT

ETHICAL LEADERSHIP: GUIDING WITH VIRTUE AND VISION

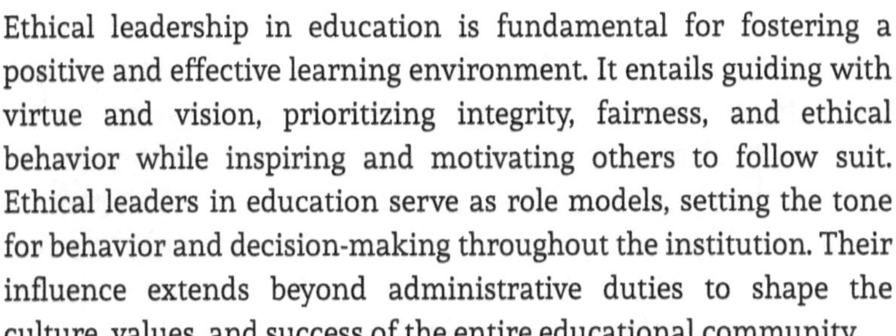

Ethical leadership in education is fundamental for fostering a positive and effective learning environment. It entails guiding with virtue and vision, prioritizing integrity, fairness, and ethical behavior while inspiring and motivating others to follow suit. Ethical leaders in education serve as role models, setting the tone for behavior and decision-making throughout the institution. Their influence extends beyond administrative duties to shape the culture, values, and success of the entire educational community.

At the heart of ethical leadership is integrity. Integrity involves being honest, transparent, and consistent in actions and decisions. Educational leaders with integrity build trust and credibility, which are crucial for creating a supportive and cohesive school environment. Trust is the foundation of effective leadership; when students, teachers, and parents trust their leaders, they are more likely to engage positively with the school community. Integrity also means upholding ethical standards even when it is challenging or inconvenient. Leaders who consistently demonstrate integrity inspire others to act ethically, fostering a culture of honesty and accountability.

Fairness is another essential component of ethical leadership. Fairness involves treating all individuals equitably, providing equal opportunities, and making decisions impartially. Educational leaders must ensure that policies and practices do not favor one group over another and that all students and staff are given the support they need to succeed. Fairness also involves being transparent about decision-making processes and providing clear, consistent criteria for evaluating performance. When leaders are fair, they build a sense of justice and trust within the school community, which is essential for maintaining morale and motivation.

Ethical leaders also demonstrate a strong sense of responsibility. They are accountable for their actions and decisions and take their duties seriously. This responsibility extends to ensuring the well-being and success of students, supporting teachers and staff, and upholding the institution's values and mission. Ethical leaders are proactive in identifying and addressing issues, whether they involve student behavior, academic performance, or administrative challenges. They take ownership of their roles and work diligently to create a positive and productive educational environment. By modeling responsibility, ethical leaders encourage others to take their responsibilities seriously and contribute to the school's success.

Vision is a critical aspect of ethical leadership. A clear, compelling vision provides direction and purpose, guiding the school community toward common goals. Ethical leaders develop and communicate a vision that reflects the institution's core values and aspirations. This vision should be inclusive and consider the diverse needs and perspectives of students, teachers, and other stakeholders. By articulating a shared vision, ethical leaders inspire and motivate others to work towards achieving the institution's goals. They also foster a sense of unity and collaboration, as everyone understands and strives to contribute to the broader mission.

Empathy and compassion are also integral to ethical leadership. Leaders who are empathetic understand and appreciate the experiences, challenges, and emotions of others. This understanding helps them to make decisions that consider the well-being of all members of the school community. Compassionate leaders show kindness and support, creating an environment where individuals feel valued and cared for. Empathy and compassion are particularly important in addressing the diverse needs of students and staff, as they ensure that everyone receives the support and encouragement they need to thrive. By demonstrating empathy and compassion, ethical leaders build strong, positive relationships and foster a sense of belonging and community.

Ethical leadership also involves ethical decision-making. Leaders are often faced with complex and challenging situations where there may be conflicting interests or values. Ethical decision-making requires leaders to carefully consider the potential impacts of their decisions, seek input from others, and weigh the pros and cons. It also involves being transparent about the decision-making process and being willing to explain and justify decisions. By making decisions that align with ethical principles and the institution's values, leaders maintain their integrity and build trust within the school community.

Professional development and continuous improvement are crucial for ethical leadership. Ethical leaders recognize that they must continually develop their skills and knowledge to effectively lead and support their school community. They seek out opportunities for professional growth, whether through formal education, training programs, or self-directed learning. By prioritizing their own development, ethical leaders set an example for others and demonstrate a commitment to lifelong learning. They also encourage and support the professional development of their staff, fostering a culture of continuous improvement and excellence.

Collaboration and teamwork are essential elements of ethical leadership. Effective leaders understand that they cannot achieve their goals alone and must work collaboratively with others. They build strong, collaborative relationships with teachers, staff, students, parents, and the broader community. This collaboration involves actively listening to others, valuing their input, and working together to find solutions to challenges. By fostering a collaborative culture, ethical leaders create an environment where everyone feels valued and empowered to contribute to the school's success.

Ethical leaders also prioritize transparency and open communication. They ensure that information is shared openly and honestly, creating an environment of trust and accountability. Transparent leaders communicate their goals, decisions, and expectations clearly and consistently. They also encourage open dialogue and feedback, creating opportunities for others to voice their opinions and concerns. By promoting transparency and open communication, ethical leaders build trust and foster a culture of openness and inclusivity.

Another important aspect of ethical leadership is the promotion of equity and inclusion. Ethical leaders are committed to creating a diverse and inclusive environment where all individuals feel valued and respected. This involves actively working to eliminate biases and barriers that may prevent individuals from achieving their full potential. Leaders must ensure that policies and practices are inclusive and equitable, providing equal opportunities for all students and staff. By promoting equity and inclusion, ethical leaders create a supportive and empowering environment where everyone can thrive.

Ethical leadership also involves advocating for the needs and interests of the school community. Leaders must be willing to speak up and take action to support their students, teachers, and staff. This advocacy may involve addressing issues such as funding, resources, or policy changes that impact the school. Ethical leaders are proactive in identifying and addressing these issues, working to create a positive and supportive environment for all. By advocating for their school community, ethical leaders demonstrate their commitment to the well-being and success of others.

Mentorship and support are also important aspects of ethical leadership. Ethical leaders serve as mentors and role models, providing guidance and support to others. They take the time to build relationships, offer encouragement, and provide constructive feedback. By serving as mentors, ethical leaders help to develop the skills and abilities of others, fostering a culture of growth and development. This mentorship and support are essential for creating a positive and empowering environment where individuals feel valued and motivated to succeed.

Ethical leaders also recognize the importance of self-care and well-being. Leading with virtue and vision requires a significant amount of energy and dedication, and leaders must take care of their own well-being to effectively support others. This involves managing stress, maintaining a healthy work-life balance, and seeking support when needed. By prioritizing their own well-being, ethical leaders set an example for others and create a culture that values and supports the well-being of all members of the school community.

Ethical leadership in education is essential for creating a positive, inclusive, and effective learning environment. It involves guiding with integrity, fairness, and a clear vision while inspiring and motivating others to follow suit. Ethical leaders build trust and credibility through their actions, foster a sense of justice and accountability, and create a supportive and collaborative culture. They prioritize the well-being and success of their school community, promote equity and inclusion, and advocate for the needs and interests of others. By modeling ethical behavior, fostering open communication, and providing mentorship and support, ethical leaders create an environment where all individuals feel valued, respected, and empowered to achieve their full potential. Through their dedication to virtue and vision, ethical leaders make a lasting impact on the lives of students, teachers, and the broader school community, helping to create a brighter and more just future for all.

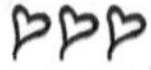

"Ethical decision-making in schools requires a
commitment to justice and equity. Educators must
consider the diverse needs of all students. Fair and
just policies create a supportive and empowering
environment."

ᗡᗡᗡ

NINE

CREATING A CULTURE OF ACCOUNTABILITY

Creating a culture of accountability in education is essential for ensuring that all members of the school community—students, teachers, administrators, and parents—are responsible for their actions and contribute positively to the learning environment. Accountability involves being answerable for one's actions, decisions, and behaviors, and it fosters a sense of ownership and commitment to the goals and values of the institution. A culture of accountability enhances trust, transparency, and integrity, which are crucial for the effective functioning of any educational institution.

At the core of a culture of accountability is the establishment of clear expectations and standards. These expectations should be communicated consistently and transparently to all members of the school community. For students, this means understanding what is expected of them in terms of behavior, academic performance, and participation. Teachers and administrators must also have clear expectations regarding their professional responsibilities, instructional practices, and interactions with students and colleagues. By setting clear standards, schools create a framework within which everyone understands their roles and responsibilities.

A key component of fostering accountability is the implementation of fair and consistent consequences for failing to meet established expectations. This involves having well-defined policies and procedures for addressing misconduct, poor performance, or breaches of ethical standards. Consequences should be applied consistently and without bias, ensuring that all individuals are held to the same standards. This consistency is crucial for maintaining fairness and trust within the school community. When students and staff know that rules and expectations are enforced uniformly, they are more likely to adhere to them.

Feedback and evaluation play a significant role in promoting accountability. Regular, constructive feedback helps individuals understand how they are performing relative to expectations and where they can improve. For students, this means receiving timely and specific feedback on their academic work and behavior. Teachers can provide feedback through assessments, classroom observations, and one-on-one discussions. Constructive feedback not only helps students improve but also reinforces the importance of meeting expectations and being accountable for their learning.

For educators, performance evaluations are a critical component of accountability. These evaluations should be comprehensive and based on multiple sources of evidence, including classroom observations, student performance data, and self-assessments. Regular evaluations provide teachers with insights into their strengths and areas for growth, helping them to refine their instructional practices and better support their students. By making the evaluation process transparent and collaborative, schools can foster a culture where continuous improvement and accountability are valued.

Professional development is another important aspect of creating a culture of accountability. Providing ongoing training and support for educators helps them stay current with best practices and enhances their ability to meet the expectations of their roles. Professional development opportunities should be aligned with the school's goals and values, and they should address the specific needs of the staff. By investing in the growth and development of educators, schools demonstrate a commitment to accountability and continuous improvement.

Accountability also involves empowering individuals to take ownership of their actions and decisions. This empowerment can be achieved by giving students and staff a voice in decision-making processes and encouraging them to take initiative. For students, this might involve opportunities to participate in school governance, lead projects, or engage in peer mentoring. When students are given a say in their education and are trusted with responsibilities, they are more likely to take ownership of their learning and behavior.

For educators, empowerment means having the autonomy to make instructional decisions that best meet the needs of their students. This autonomy should be balanced with accountability measures that ensure teachers are meeting professional standards and contributing to the school's goals. By trusting teachers to use their professional judgment and providing them with the support they need, schools can foster a sense of responsibility and commitment to high standards.

Transparency is essential for creating a culture of accountability. Open communication about expectations, policies, and performance helps build trust and ensures that everyone understands the criteria by which they are being judged. Schools should regularly communicate with students, parents, and staff about goals, progress, and areas for improvement. This communication can take the form of newsletters, meetings, reports, and informal conversations. By keeping everyone informed and involved, schools can create a sense of shared responsibility and commitment to the institution's success.

Another critical aspect of accountability is the role of leadership. School leaders set the tone for the entire institution by modeling accountable behavior and holding themselves to the same standards as everyone else. Leaders should demonstrate transparency, integrity, and a commitment to continuous improvement. By being accountable in their actions and decisions, leaders inspire others to do the same. Leadership also involves creating systems and structures that support accountability, such as clear policies, regular evaluations, and opportunities for professional development.

Collaboration is an important element in fostering a culture of accountability. When individuals work together towards common goals, they are more likely to hold each other accountable and support each other's growth. Collaborative practices can include team teaching, professional learning communities, and peer observations. These practices provide opportunities for educators to share best practices, give and receive feedback, and collectively address challenges. Collaboration enhances accountability by creating a supportive environment where everyone is working towards the same objectives.

In addition to internal accountability measures, schools should also be accountable to external stakeholders, including parents, the community, and governing bodies. This involves regularly reporting on the school's performance, progress towards goals, and how resources are being used. Transparency with external stakeholders helps build trust and ensures that the school is meeting its obligations to the wider community. Engaging with external stakeholders also provides valuable perspectives and insights that can inform the school's practices and policies.

Creating a culture of accountability also requires addressing and mitigating any obstacles that may hinder accountability. This might involve addressing issues such as inequitable resource distribution, lack of support for staff, or biases in evaluation processes. By identifying and addressing these obstacles, schools can create a more equitable and supportive environment where everyone has the opportunity to succeed and be accountable.

Recognizing and celebrating success is another important aspect of fostering accountability. Acknowledging the achievements and efforts of students, teachers, and staff reinforces the importance of meeting expectations and encourages continued commitment to excellence. This recognition can take many forms, such as awards, public acknowledgments, or personal notes of appreciation. Celebrating success helps build a positive school culture where individuals feel valued and motivated to contribute their best.

Creating a culture of accountability is not a one-time effort but an ongoing process that requires continuous reflection and improvement. Schools should regularly assess their accountability practices and seek feedback from all members of the school community. This reflection helps identify areas for improvement and ensures that accountability measures remain effective and relevant. By committing to continuous improvement, schools can sustain a culture of accountability that supports long-term success.

Creating a culture of accountability in education is essential for fostering a positive and effective learning environment. It involves establishing clear expectations and standards, providing fair and consistent consequences, and offering regular feedback and evaluation. Professional development, empowerment, and transparency are crucial for promoting accountability among students and staff.

Leadership plays a key role in modeling accountable behavior and creating systems that support accountability. Collaboration, engagement with external stakeholders, and addressing obstacles are also important elements. Recognizing and celebrating success reinforces the importance of accountability, and continuous reflection and improvement ensure that accountability measures remain effective. By prioritizing accountability, schools can create a culture of trust, integrity, and excellence, where all members of the school community are committed to their roles and responsibilities and contribute positively to the institution's goals.

ᠵᠵᠵ

"Modeling ethical behavior is the most powerful teaching tool. Students learn integrity and respect by observing their educators. Actions speak louder than words in the journey towards ethical excellence."

ᗐᗐᗐ

TEN

Conflict Resolution: Navigating Ethical Dilemmas in Schools

Conflict resolution and navigating ethical dilemmas in schools are vital components of maintaining a harmonious and effective educational environment. Schools are diverse communities where individuals from various backgrounds, cultures, and perspectives come together, making conflict inevitable. Effective conflict resolution involves addressing disputes in a manner that is fair, respectful, and constructive, ensuring that all parties feel heard and valued. Ethical dilemmas, on the other hand, require careful consideration and decision-making, often involving complex issues with no clear right or wrong answers. Navigating these dilemmas requires a strong ethical foundation, critical thinking, and a commitment to the core values of the educational institution.

Conflicts in schools can arise from a variety of sources, including misunderstandings, competition for resources, differing values and beliefs, and interpersonal issues. When conflicts are left unresolved, they can escalate, leading to a negative impact on the school climate, student performance, and overall well-being. Therefore, it is essential for educators, administrators, and students to have the skills and strategies necessary to address and resolve conflicts effectively. This begins with fostering a culture of open communication and mutual respect, where individuals feel comfortable expressing their concerns and perspectives without fear of retaliation or judgment.

Active listening is a fundamental skill in conflict resolution. It involves fully concentrating on the speaker, understanding their message, and responding thoughtfully. Active listening helps to de-escalate tensions by showing that all parties' views are valued and taken seriously. When individuals feel heard, they are more likely to engage in a constructive dialogue and work towards a resolution. Educators and administrators should model active listening and encourage students to practice it in their interactions with peers.

Mediation is another effective conflict resolution strategy that can be employed in schools. Mediation involves a neutral third party who facilitates a discussion between conflicting parties to help them reach a mutually agreeable solution. This process encourages open communication, problem-solving, and compromise. School counselors, trained teachers, or external mediators can play this role, ensuring that the mediation process is fair and unbiased. Mediation not only resolves the immediate conflict but also teaches valuable skills in negotiation and cooperation that students can use in future disputes.

Restorative practices are increasingly being used in schools to address conflicts and repair relationships. These practices focus on accountability, making amends, and rebuilding trust. Restorative circles, for example, bring together those involved in a conflict to discuss the impact of their actions, express their feelings, and collaboratively develop a plan to make things right. This approach emphasizes empathy and understanding, helping students learn from their mistakes and develop a deeper sense of responsibility towards others.

When it comes to ethical dilemmas, schools face challenges that require careful consideration and balanced decision-making. Ethical dilemmas often involve situations where there are competing values or interests, and the right course of action is not immediately clear. Navigating these dilemmas requires a strong ethical framework and a commitment to the principles of fairness, integrity, and respect.

One common ethical dilemma in schools involves issues of fairness and equity. For instance, educators may face decisions about how to allocate limited resources, such as funding, time, or support services, in a way that is fair to all students. These decisions can be particularly challenging when considering the diverse needs and backgrounds of students. To navigate such dilemmas, schools should establish clear criteria and processes for decision-making that are transparent and inclusive. Involving stakeholders, including students, parents, and teachers, in the decision-making process can help ensure that diverse perspectives are considered and that the final decision is fair and just.

Another ethical dilemma that schools often encounter is related to student discipline. Balancing the need to maintain order and safety with the principles of fairness and compassion can be difficult. Zero-tolerance policies, for example, can sometimes lead to disproportionate consequences for minor infractions, potentially causing harm to students' educational and emotional well-being. To address this, schools should adopt disciplinary practices that are restorative rather than punitive, focusing on understanding the root causes of behavior, promoting positive behavior, and providing support to help students make better choices in the future.

Privacy and confidentiality issues also present ethical dilemmas in schools. Educators and administrators must balance the need to protect students' privacy with the need to ensure their safety and well-being. For example, when a student discloses sensitive information about abuse or mental health issues, school staff must decide how to handle this information in a way that respects the student's privacy while also fulfilling their legal and ethical obligations to report and address the issue. Clear policies and training on confidentiality and mandatory reporting can help school staff navigate these complex situations.

Technology use in schools has introduced new ethical dilemmas related to digital citizenship, online behavior, and data privacy. Schools must address issues such as cyberbullying, inappropriate content, and the ethical use of digital resources. Educators should teach students about responsible online behavior, the importance of protecting personal information, and the consequences of unethical actions online. Schools should also implement robust data privacy policies to protect students' personal information and ensure that technology is used ethically and responsibly.

Navigating ethical dilemmas also requires a commitment to ongoing reflection and professional development. Educators and administrators should engage in regular discussions and training on ethical issues, staying informed about best practices and emerging challenges. Ethical decision-making is a skill that can be developed through practice and critical thinking. By fostering a culture of ethical awareness and reflection, schools can better prepare staff to handle dilemmas thoughtfully and effectively.

Leadership plays a crucial role in promoting ethical behavior and conflict resolution within schools. School leaders set the tone for the entire institution by modeling ethical behavior, making decisions transparently, and holding themselves and others accountable. Ethical leaders create an environment where open dialogue, mutual respect, and integrity are valued. They support staff in developing their conflict resolution and ethical decision-making skills and provide the necessary resources and training to navigate complex issues. By prioritizing ethical leadership, schools can build a strong foundation for addressing conflicts and dilemmas constructively.

Collaboration and community involvement are essential for effective conflict resolution and ethical decision-making. Schools should engage parents, community members, and external organizations in addressing issues and finding solutions. Community involvement provides additional perspectives and resources, enhancing the school's ability to navigate conflicts and dilemmas. Collaborative efforts also build stronger relationships between the school and the community, fostering a sense of shared responsibility and commitment to the well-being of students.

Creating a culture of accountability is integral to conflict resolution and ethical behavior. Accountability involves being responsible for one's actions and decisions and being willing to address and learn from mistakes. Schools should establish clear expectations and standards for behavior and decision-making, and hold individuals accountable in a fair and consistent manner. Accountability mechanisms, such as regular performance evaluations, feedback systems, and transparent reporting processes, help ensure that everyone in the school community is committed to upholding ethical standards and resolving conflicts constructively.

Student involvement in conflict resolution and ethical decision-making is also important. Empowering students to take an active role in addressing conflicts and dilemmas fosters a sense of ownership and responsibility. Schools can provide opportunities for students to participate in peer mediation programs, student councils, and other leadership activities that promote ethical behavior and conflict resolution skills. By involving students in these processes, schools help them develop critical thinking, empathy, and problem-solving skills that will serve them well throughout their lives.

In conclusion, conflict resolution and navigating ethical dilemmas are critical components of maintaining a positive and effective educational environment. Addressing conflicts constructively involves fostering open communication, practicing active listening, and employing strategies such as mediation and restorative practices. Navigating ethical dilemmas requires a strong ethical framework, transparency, and a commitment to the principles of fairness, integrity, and respect.

Schools must also engage in ongoing reflection, professional development, and community collaboration to effectively address these challenges. Leadership and accountability are essential for promoting ethical behavior and resolving conflicts, while student involvement empowers young people to take responsibility for their actions and contribute to a positive school culture. By prioritizing conflict resolution and ethical decision-making, schools can create a harmonious and inclusive environment where all members feel valued, respected, and capable of achieving their full potential.

ᐅᐅᐅ

"Professional development focused on ethics equips educators to handle complex dilemmas. Continuous learning and reflection are essential. This commitment enhances the overall ethical climate of the school."

❦❦❦

ELEVEN

THE IMPACT OF ETHICAL EXCELLENCE ON STUDENT ACHIEVEMENT

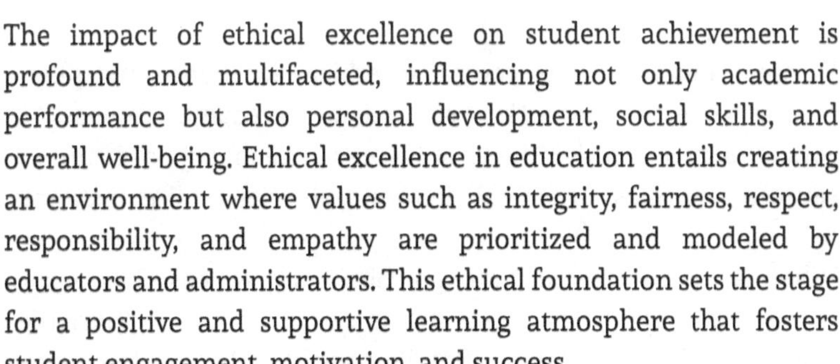

The impact of ethical excellence on student achievement is profound and multifaceted, influencing not only academic performance but also personal development, social skills, and overall well-being. Ethical excellence in education entails creating an environment where values such as integrity, fairness, respect, responsibility, and empathy are prioritized and modeled by educators and administrators. This ethical foundation sets the stage for a positive and supportive learning atmosphere that fosters student engagement, motivation, and success.

When schools prioritize ethical excellence, they cultivate a culture of trust and respect. Trust is fundamental to any effective educational environment, as it forms the basis of positive relationships between students and teachers. When students trust their teachers, they are more likely to engage in the learning process, participate actively in class discussions, and seek help when needed.

This trust also encourages students to take academic risks, such as attempting challenging tasks and expressing their ideas without fear of ridicule or retribution. In turn, these behaviors contribute to deeper learning and higher academic achievement.

Respect is another critical component of ethical excellence that significantly impacts student achievement. In a respectful classroom environment, students feel valued and acknowledged for their unique perspectives and contributions. This sense of respect fosters a positive self-image and self-worth, which are essential for academic motivation and perseverance.

When students feel respected, they are more likely to respect others, creating a collaborative and supportive classroom culture. This mutual respect enhances the learning experience, as students are more willing to work together, share ideas, and support each other's academic growth.

Fairness and equity are central to ethical excellence and play a crucial role in promoting student achievement. Fairness in education means providing all students with equal opportunities to succeed, regardless of their background, abilities, or circumstances.

When schools implement fair policies and practices, they ensure that every student has access to the resources and support they need to reach their full potential. This might include differentiated instruction, personalized learning plans, and additional academic support for students who need it. By addressing the diverse needs of students, schools can help close achievement gaps and ensure that all students have the opportunity to succeed.

Equity in education also involves creating an inclusive environment where all students feel a sense of belonging. This inclusivity is essential for student engagement and achievement, as it ensures that students feel accepted and valued for who they are.

An inclusive environment promotes positive social interactions, reduces instances of bullying and discrimination, and fosters a sense of community and support. When students feel included and accepted, they are more likely to participate actively in their education, take pride in their work, and strive for academic excellence.

Responsibility is another key aspect of ethical excellence that influences student achievement. When students are taught to take responsibility for their actions and learning, they develop important skills such as self-regulation, time management, and goal-setting. These skills are critical for academic success, as they enable students to stay focused, manage their workload effectively, and persist in the face of challenges. Educators can promote responsibility by setting clear expectations, providing guidance and support, and encouraging students to take ownership of their learning. By fostering a sense of responsibility, schools help students develop the intrinsic motivation and self-discipline needed for academic achievement.

Empathy and compassion are also integral to ethical excellence and have a significant impact on student achievement. When educators model empathy and compassion, they create a supportive and caring classroom environment where students feel understood and valued. This emotional support is crucial for student well-being and academic success, as it helps students cope with stress, build resilience, and stay motivated.

Additionally, teaching students to empathize with others promotes positive social interactions and reduces conflict, creating a more harmonious and productive learning environment. By fostering empathy and compassion, schools help students develop the emotional intelligence and social skills needed for success in both academic and personal realms.

The impact of ethical excellence on student achievement is also evident in the development of critical thinking and ethical decision-making skills. When schools emphasize ethical behavior and moral reasoning, they encourage students to think critically about their actions and the consequences of their choices. This critical thinking is essential for academic success, as it enables students to analyze information, evaluate different perspectives, and make informed decisions. Ethical decision-making skills also prepare students for the complex challenges they will face in the future, both in their personal lives and professional careers. By promoting ethical excellence, schools help students develop the cognitive and ethical skills needed for success in all areas of life.

Moreover, ethical excellence contributes to a positive school culture that supports student achievement. A school culture that prioritizes ethical values creates a safe and supportive environment where students can thrive. This positive culture is characterized by open communication, mutual respect, and a shared commitment to the school's values and goals. When students feel part of a positive and supportive school community, they are more likely to be engaged in their learning, attend school regularly, and strive for academic success. Additionally, a positive school culture fosters a sense of pride and belonging, which further motivates students to achieve their best.

The role of educators in promoting ethical excellence and its impact on student achievement cannot be overstated. Teachers who model ethical behavior, provide a supportive and caring environment, and set high expectations for their students play a crucial role in fostering student achievement. When educators demonstrate integrity, fairness, and empathy, they inspire students to adopt these values and behaviors in their own lives. This modeling is particularly important for young students, who are still developing their moral and ethical frameworks. By serving as positive role models, educators help students develop the values and behaviors that are essential for academic and personal success.

Parental and community involvement is also important for promoting ethical excellence and supporting student achievement. When parents and community members are engaged in the educational process, they reinforce the values and behaviors promoted by the school. This collaboration creates a consistent and supportive environment for students, both at school and at home. Schools can encourage parental and community involvement by fostering open communication, providing opportunities for engagement, and building strong partnerships. By working together, schools, parents, and communities can create a comprehensive support system that promotes ethical excellence and student achievement.

The impact of ethical excellence on student achievement is significant and far-reaching. Ethical excellence in education involves creating an environment where values such as integrity, fairness, respect, responsibility, and empathy are prioritized and modeled. These values foster a culture of trust and respect, which is essential for student engagement and motivation.

Fairness and equity ensure that all students have equal opportunities to succeed, while responsibility and empathy promote positive social interactions and emotional support. Ethical excellence also contributes to the development of critical thinking and ethical decision-making skills, which are crucial for academic and personal success.

Additionally, a positive school culture that prioritizes ethical values creates a safe and supportive environment where students can thrive. Educators play a key role in promoting ethical excellence, serving as role models and providing a supportive and caring environment. Parental and community involvement further reinforces these values, creating a comprehensive support system for students. By prioritizing ethical excellence, schools can significantly enhance student achievement and prepare students for success in all areas of life.

ᢂᢂᢂ

"Real-life case studies of ethical excellence inspire and guide us. They show the transformative power of integrity and fairness. Learning from these examples strengthens our resolve to uphold ethical standards."

❦❦❦

TWELVE

Encouraging Ethical Behavior through Curriculum Design

Encouraging ethical behavior through curriculum design is an essential strategy for fostering a generation of students who are not only academically proficient but also morally and socially responsible. Curriculum design that incorporates ethical considerations helps students develop a strong moral compass, critical thinking skills, and the ability to navigate complex social and ethical issues. This approach to education involves integrating ethical principles and discussions into various subjects, creating opportunities for students to engage with ethical dilemmas, and providing a framework that supports the development of ethical reasoning and behavior.

One of the fundamental aspects of encouraging ethical behavior through curriculum design is the intentional inclusion of ethical principles and values across all subjects. Rather than treating ethics as a standalone topic, it should be woven into the fabric of the entire curriculum. This integration ensures that students encounter ethical considerations in various contexts and understand their relevance to different fields of study. For instance, in science classes, discussions about the ethical implications of scientific research, environmental conservation, and technological advancements can help students appreciate the moral responsibilities that come with scientific knowledge. In literature classes, analyzing characters' decisions and moral conflicts in novels and plays provides a rich ground for exploring ethical themes and human behavior.

Critical thinking is another vital component of a curriculum designed to encourage ethical behavior. Developing students' critical thinking skills enables them to analyze and evaluate complex ethical issues thoughtfully and independently. By engaging students in discussions, debates, and case studies, educators can help them learn to consider multiple perspectives, weigh evidence, and make reasoned ethical decisions. For example, history classes can explore ethical dilemmas faced by historical figures, allowing students to assess the context, motivations, and consequences of their actions. Such activities not only enhance students' understanding of historical events but also encourage them to think critically about the ethical dimensions of human behavior.

Ethical behavior can also be encouraged through experiential learning opportunities. Service-learning projects, internships, and community engagement activities provide students with hands-on experiences that connect academic learning with real-world ethical challenges. These experiences help students understand the impact of their actions on others and develop a sense of social responsibility. For instance, a service-learning project that involves working with a local charity can teach students about the importance of empathy, compassion, and civic engagement. By reflecting on their experiences, students can gain insights into their values and ethical beliefs, which can guide their future behavior.

Role-playing and simulations are effective methods for teaching ethical behavior within the curriculum. These interactive activities allow students to step into different roles and navigate ethical dilemmas in a controlled environment. Through role-playing, students can practice ethical decision-making, consider the consequences of various actions, and develop empathy by seeing issues from different perspectives. For example, a business class might simulate a corporate board meeting where students must decide on an ethical issue, such as environmental sustainability or labor practices. Such simulations can help students understand the complexities of ethical decision-making in professional contexts and prepare them for real-world challenges.

Reflection is a critical component of encouraging ethical behavior through curriculum design. Reflective practices, such as journaling, group discussions, and personal essays, provide students with opportunities to consider their values, experiences, and ethical beliefs. Reflection helps students internalize ethical principles and develop a deeper understanding of their moral responsibilities. Educators can incorporate reflective activities into the curriculum by asking students to write about their responses to ethical dilemmas, discuss their thoughts and feelings about certain ethical issues, or reflect on their behavior in various situations. By regularly engaging in reflection, students can develop a habit of self-assessment and ethical reasoning that will serve them throughout their lives.

Collaboration and peer learning are also important aspects of a curriculum designed to encourage ethical behavior. Working in groups allows students to discuss ethical issues, share diverse perspectives, and develop interpersonal skills such as communication, negotiation, and conflict resolution. Collaborative projects can involve ethical decision-making tasks where students must work together to find solutions to complex problems. For instance, a social studies class might investigate a current social issue, such as income inequality or climate change, and propose ethical solutions as a group. These activities help students learn to appreciate different viewpoints, work cooperatively, and make collective ethical decisions.

Teachers play a crucial role in modeling ethical behavior and guiding students in their ethical development. Educators must demonstrate integrity, fairness, and respect in their interactions with students and colleagues. By setting a positive example, teachers can influence students' attitudes and behaviors. Additionally, teachers should create a classroom environment that encourages open dialogue, critical thinking, and respect for diverse opinions. This environment fosters a culture of ethical inquiry where students feel comfortable discussing ethical issues and exploring their beliefs.

Assessing students' ethical development is another important aspect of curriculum design. Traditional assessments, such as tests and quizzes, may not fully capture students' understanding and application of ethical principles. Instead, educators should use a variety of assessment methods that allow students to demonstrate their ethical reasoning and decision-making skills. These methods might include written reflections, case study analyses, group projects, and presentations. By using diverse assessment techniques, educators can gain a more comprehensive understanding of students' ethical development and provide feedback that supports their growth.

Parental and community involvement is essential for reinforcing the ethical principles taught in the classroom. Schools can engage parents and community members by providing information about the curriculum's ethical components and offering opportunities for involvement in ethical discussions and activities. For example, schools might host workshops, seminars, or discussion panels on ethical issues, inviting parents and community members to participate. This involvement helps create a consistent and supportive environment for students, both at school and at home, and reinforces the importance of ethical behavior in all areas of life.

Professional development for educators is also crucial for the successful implementation of a curriculum that encourages ethical behavior. Teachers need training and support to effectively integrate ethical principles into their teaching and to facilitate discussions about complex ethical issues. Professional development opportunities should include workshops on ethical theories, strategies for teaching ethics, and methods for assessing students' ethical development. By investing in the professional growth of educators, schools can ensure that they are equipped to guide students in their ethical development.

Technology can be a powerful tool for teaching ethical behavior and enhancing the curriculum. Digital resources, such as online case studies, interactive simulations, and educational games, can provide engaging and dynamic ways for students to explore ethical issues. Technology also enables students to access diverse perspectives and collaborate with peers from different backgrounds, fostering a global understanding of ethical principles. Educators should leverage technology to create innovative and effective learning experiences that promote ethical behavior and critical thinking.

Cultural competence is an important aspect of ethical behavior that should be integrated into the curriculum. Students should be exposed to diverse cultures, perspectives, and experiences to develop empathy, respect, and understanding for others. Curriculum design should include opportunities for students to learn about different cultural traditions, values, and ethical systems. This exposure helps students appreciate the complexity of ethical issues and develop a more inclusive and global perspective. By promoting cultural competence, schools can prepare students to navigate an increasingly interconnected and diverse world.

Encouraging ethical behavior through curriculum design also involves creating opportunities for students to take ethical action. Schools should provide students with chances to apply their ethical learning in real-world contexts, such as through community service projects, internships, and advocacy efforts.

These experiences help students see the impact of their actions and develop a sense of responsibility and agency. For example, a school might partner with local organizations to create service-learning projects that address community needs, such as environmental conservation, poverty alleviation, or public health. By taking ethical action, students can make a positive difference in their communities and develop a lifelong commitment to ethical behavior.

Encouraging ethical behavior through curriculum design is essential for fostering a generation of students who are morally and socially responsible. Integrating ethical principles and discussions into various subjects, developing critical thinking skills, providing experiential learning opportunities, and promoting reflection and collaboration are key strategies for achieving this goal. Teachers play a crucial role in modeling ethical behavior and guiding students in their ethical development, while diverse assessment methods help evaluate students' progress.

Parental and community inovolvement, professional development for educators, the use of technology, and promoting cultural competence are also important aspects of a comprehensive approach to ethical education. By creating a curriculum that encourages ethical behavior, schools can help students develop the values, skills, and commitment needed to navigate complex ethical issues and make a positive impact in their communities and the world.

❦❦❦

"Fostering a sense of community within schools encourages collaboration and mutual support. A strong community values and promotes ethical behavior. Together, we can create environments where everyone thrives."

ᗡᗡᗡ

THIRTEEN

ROLE MODELS IN EDUCATION: CELEBRATING EXEMPLARY EDUCATORS

Role models in education play a pivotal role in shaping the attitudes, behaviors, and aspirations of students. Celebrating exemplary educators highlights the profound impact that dedicated and passionate teachers have on the lives of their students. These educators serve as beacons of inspiration, demonstrating the values of integrity, perseverance, and a commitment to lifelong learning. Their influence extends beyond the classroom, leaving lasting impressions that guide students throughout their academic journeys and into their adult lives.

Exemplary educators possess a unique combination of qualities that set them apart as role models. They demonstrate a deep passion for their subject matter and a genuine enthusiasm for teaching. This passion is infectious, inspiring students to engage with the material and develop a love for learning.

When teachers are enthusiastic about their subjects, students are more likely to be curious, ask questions, and explore topics in greater depth. This enthusiasm creates a dynamic and stimulating learning environment where students feel motivated to achieve their best.

Moreover, exemplary educators exhibit a high level of professionalism and integrity. They are committed to maintaining ethical standards in their teaching practices, treating all students with fairness and respect. These educators understand the importance of modeling ethical behavior, knowing that their actions set a powerful example for their students. By demonstrating honesty, accountability, and respect, they create a classroom culture based on trust and mutual respect.

This ethical foundation is crucial for fostering a positive and inclusive learning environment where all students feel valued and supported.

Compassion and empathy are also defining characteristics of exemplary educators. These teachers recognize the diverse needs and challenges that students face and respond with understanding and support. They take the time to listen to their students, offering encouragement and assistance when needed.

This compassionate approach helps to build strong relationships between teachers and students, creating a sense of community and belonging. When students feel that their teachers genuinely care about their well-being, they are more likely to be engaged and motivated in their studies.

Exemplary educators are also innovative and adaptable. They

continuously seek out new teaching methods and strategies to enhance their instruction and meet the diverse needs of their students. These teachers are not afraid to experiment with new technologies, incorporate creative activities, or modify their teaching approaches to better engage students.

This adaptability ensures that learning remains relevant and engaging, helping students to develop critical thinking skills and a love for learning. By staying current with educational trends and best practices, exemplary educators ensure that their teaching is effective and impactful.

One of the most significant ways that exemplary educators serve as role models is through their commitment to lifelong learning. These teachers are dedicated to their own professional growth and development, continually seeking out opportunities to expand their knowledge and skills. They attend workshops, pursue advanced degrees, participate in professional learning communities, and stay informed about the latest research in education.

This commitment to continuous improvement not only enhances their teaching but also demonstrates to students the importance of lifelong learning. When students see their teachers actively engaged in their own learning, they are more likely to adopt a similar mindset and pursue their own educational goals with determination and enthusiasm.

The impact of exemplary educators extends beyond academic achievement. These teachers also play a crucial role in the personal and social development of their students. By modeling positive behaviors and attitudes, they help students develop important life skills such as resilience, perseverance, and effective communication. Exemplary educators encourage students to set high standards for themselves, to work hard, and to strive for excellence in all areas of their lives.

They help students to build self-confidence and a sense of agency, empowering them to overcome challenges and pursue their dreams.

Celebrating exemplary educators is essential for recognizing their contributions and inspiring others to follow in their footsteps. By highlighting the achievements and impact of these teachers, schools and communities can promote a culture of excellence in education.

This recognition can take many forms, such as awards, public acknowledgments, and opportunities for professional advancement. Celebrating exemplary educators not only honors their hard work and dedication but also raises awareness of the critical role that teachers play in shaping the future.

Moreover, celebrating exemplary educators can help to attract and retain high-quality teachers. Teaching is a demanding and often underappreciated profession, and recognition of excellence can provide much-needed motivation and support. When teachers feel valued and appreciated, they are more likely to stay in the profession and continue to contribute to the success of their students. Additionally, highlighting the achievements of exemplary educators can inspire others to pursue careers in education, helping to ensure that schools are staffed with passionate and skilled teachers.

Mentorship is another important aspect of the role that exemplary educators play. Experienced teachers can serve as mentors to new or less experienced colleagues, providing guidance, support, and encouragement. This mentorship helps to build a strong professional community where teachers collaborate, share best practices, and support each other's growth.

Mentorship also helps to ensure that high standards of teaching are maintained and that the values and principles of exemplary educators are passed on to future generations of teachers. By serving as mentors, exemplary educators contribute to the overall quality of education and help to create a positive and supportive school culture.

Exemplary educators also have a significant impact on their communities. They often engage in activities outside the classroom that benefit their students and the wider community. This might include organizing community service projects, participating in local events, or advocating for educational initiatives and policies. By taking an active role in their communities, these educators demonstrate the importance of civic engagement and social responsibility. They help students to understand that learning is not confined to the classroom but is a lifelong endeavor that involves contributing to the well-being of others.

Furthermore, exemplary educators often collaborate with parents and families to support student learning and development. They recognize that education is a partnership between the school and the home and work to build strong relationships with parents. This collaboration might involve regular communication, parent-teacher conferences, and opportunities for parents to be involved in school activities.

By engaging parents in the educational process, exemplary educators help to create a supportive network that enhances student achievement and well-being. This partnership also reinforces the values and behaviors that are being taught in the classroom, providing students with a consistent and supportive environment for learning.

Role models in education, particularly exemplary educators, have a profound and lasting impact on their students and communities. These educators inspire and motivate students through their passion, professionalism, integrity, compassion, and commitment to lifelong learning.

They create positive and inclusive classroom environments that foster academic achievement and personal growth. Celebrating exemplary educators highlights their contributions and promotes a culture of excellence in education. Recognition of these teachers helps to attract and retain high-quality educators and inspires others to pursue careers in teaching.

By serving as mentors and engaging with their communities, exemplary educators contribute to the overall quality of education and the well-being of their students. Their influence extends far beyond the classroom, shaping the attitudes, behaviors, and aspirations of their students and leaving a lasting legacy that benefits society as a whole.

ᚦᚦᚦ

"The pursuit of ethical excellence in education benefits individuals and society as a whole. It prepares students for responsible citizenship. By nurturing ethical behavior, we contribute to a better world."

▷▷▷

FOURTEEN

ETHICAL DECISION-MAKING: TOOLS AND TECHNIQUES FOR EDUCATORS

Ethical decision-making is a crucial aspect of the educational profession, requiring educators to navigate complex and often challenging situations with integrity, fairness, and a commitment to the best interests of their students. The ability to make sound ethical decisions is essential for maintaining trust, fostering a positive learning environment, and upholding the values of the educational institution. To support educators in this important aspect of their role, various tools and techniques can be employed to enhance their ethical decision-making capabilities.

One of the foundational tools for ethical decision-making is a well-defined ethical framework. This framework provides a structured approach for analyzing and resolving ethical dilemmas. It typically involves identifying the relevant ethical principles, considering the potential impacts of different courses of action, and evaluating the consistency of these actions with the values and mission of the educational institution. By having a clear ethical framework in place, educators can systematically approach complex situations and make decisions that align with their professional and ethical obligations.

Critical thinking is another essential tool for ethical decision-making. Critical thinking involves the ability to analyze information, evaluate different perspectives, and consider the implications of various options. Educators can enhance their critical thinking skills by engaging in reflective practice, seeking out diverse viewpoints, and participating in professional development opportunities that focus on ethical reasoning. By developing their critical thinking abilities, educators can more effectively navigate the nuances of ethical dilemmas and make informed, reasoned decisions.

Collaboration and consultation are also valuable techniques for ethical decision-making. When faced with an ethical dilemma, educators can benefit from discussing the issue with colleagues, administrators, or other trusted individuals. This collaborative approach allows educators to gain insights from different perspectives, consider alternative solutions, and ensure that their decisions are well-informed and balanced. Schools can support this process by fostering a culture of open communication and providing opportunities for educators to engage in ethical discussions and peer consultation.

Professional codes of ethics serve as important guides for ethical decision-making in education. These codes outline the core values and principles that educators are expected to uphold, such as integrity, fairness, respect, and responsibility. By adhering to these codes, educators can ensure that their decisions are aligned with the standards of their profession. Familiarity with professional codes of ethics can also provide educators with a sense of confidence and clarity when navigating ethical challenges, as they have a clear reference point for what constitutes appropriate conduct.

Ethical decision-making also involves considering the welfare and best interests of students. This student-centered approach requires educators to prioritize the well-being, safety, and development of their students in all decisions. When faced with an ethical dilemma, educators should ask themselves how their actions will impact their students and whether these actions will support or hinder their students' growth and success. This focus on student welfare helps to ensure that decisions are made with compassion and a commitment to fostering a positive and supportive learning environment.

Empathy is a powerful tool for ethical decision-making. Empathy involves understanding and sharing the feelings and perspectives of others. By cultivating empathy, educators can better appreciate the experiences and needs of their students, colleagues, and other stakeholders. This deeper understanding can inform their decision-making process, helping them to consider the emotional and social implications of their actions. Empathy also promotes a compassionate approach to resolving ethical dilemmas, ensuring that decisions are made with sensitivity and respect for all individuals involved.

Reflective practice is another technique that supports ethical decision-making. Reflective practice involves regularly examining one's actions, decisions, and experiences to gain insights and identify areas for improvement. Educators can engage in reflective practice by keeping a journal, participating in reflective discussions with colleagues, or setting aside time for personal contemplation. By reflecting on their ethical decision-making processes, educators can learn from past experiences, recognize patterns, and develop strategies for handling similar situations in the future. This ongoing reflection helps to build ethical awareness and enhances the educator's ability to make sound decisions.

Scenario-based training and role-playing exercises are effective methods for developing ethical decision-making skills. These activities provide educators with opportunities to practice navigating ethical dilemmas in a controlled and supportive environment. By working through realistic scenarios and role-playing different roles, educators can explore various approaches to resolving ethical issues, receive feedback, and refine their decision-making strategies. Scenario-based training also helps educators to anticipate potential challenges and prepare for real-world situations, increasing their confidence and competence in handling ethical dilemmas.

Clear policies and procedures are essential for guiding ethical decision-making in educational institutions. Schools should establish and communicate policies that outline the expected standards of conduct, the process for addressing ethical concerns, and the consequences of unethical behavior. These policies provide a framework for consistent and fair decision-making, ensuring that all members of the school community understand their responsibilities and the principles that guide their actions. By having clear policies in place, schools can support educators in making ethical decisions and provide a basis for accountability.

Support from leadership is critical for fostering ethical decision-making among educators. School leaders play a key role in setting the tone for ethical behavior and modeling ethical decision-making. They can support their staff by providing resources, training, and guidance on ethical issues, as well as creating a culture of transparency and accountability. When school leaders demonstrate a commitment to ethical principles and support their staff in navigating ethical dilemmas, they help to build a strong foundation for ethical decision-making throughout the institution.

Community engagement is another important aspect of ethical decision-making in education. Educators should consider the values, expectations, and needs of the broader community when making decisions. By involving parents, community members, and other stakeholders in discussions about ethical issues, schools can ensure that their decisions reflect the diverse perspectives and values of the community they serve. Community engagement also promotes transparency and trust, as stakeholders feel that their voices are heard and respected.

Professional development opportunities focused on ethics and ethical decision-making are essential for supporting educators in this area. Schools should offer workshops, seminars, and training sessions that explore ethical theories, principles, and practical strategies for navigating ethical dilemmas. These professional development opportunities provide educators with the knowledge and skills they need to make informed and ethical decisions. They also create a space for educators to discuss ethical challenges, share experiences, and learn from one another.

Creating an environment that encourages ethical behavior and decision-making requires a holistic approach. Schools should integrate ethical considerations into all aspects of their operations, from curriculum design and teaching practices to administrative policies and community engagement. By embedding ethical principles into the fabric of the school culture, educators are constantly reminded of the importance of ethical behavior and are supported in their efforts to make ethical decisions.

Ethical decision-making is a critical component of the educational profession, requiring educators to navigate complex situations with integrity, fairness, and a commitment to the best interests of their students. Various tools and techniques can enhance educators' ethical decision-making capabilities, including well-defined ethical frameworks, critical thinking, collaboration, professional codes of ethics, empathy, reflective practice, scenario-based training, clear policies, leadership support, community engagement, and professional development.

By employing these tools and techniques, educators can effectively address ethical dilemmas and make decisions that uphold the values and mission of their educational institution. Creating a culture that prioritizes ethical decision-making requires a comprehensive and integrated approach, ensuring that ethical principles are embedded in all aspects of the school's operations. Through this commitment to ethical excellence, educators can foster a positive and supportive learning environment that promotes the well-being and success of all students.

ᎠᎠᎠ

"Ethical education requires a holistic approach, integrating values into every aspect of school life. This includes curriculum, leadership, and community involvement. A comprehensive strategy ensures lasting impact."

FIFTEEN

FOSTERING A SENSE OF COMMUNITY IN SCHOOLS

Fostering a sense of community in schools is essential for creating an environment where students, teachers, and staff feel connected, supported, and valued. A strong sense of community enhances student engagement, academic achievement, and overall well-being. It also promotes positive relationships, mutual respect, and a collaborative spirit that benefits the entire school. Achieving this requires intentional efforts to build relationships, create inclusive environments, and encourage participation from all members of the school community.

At the heart of fostering a sense of community in schools is the establishment of strong, positive relationships among students, teachers, and staff. Building these relationships starts with creating a welcoming and inclusive atmosphere where everyone feels valued and respected. Teachers play a crucial role in this by modeling kindness, empathy, and respect in their interactions with students and colleagues. By showing genuine interest in their students' lives, teachers can build trust and rapport, which are fundamental for a strong community.

One effective way to build relationships and foster a sense of community is through regular, meaningful interactions. This can be achieved through activities that encourage collaboration and teamwork, such as group projects, classroom discussions, and peer mentoring programs. These activities provide opportunities for students to work together, learn from each other, and develop a sense of camaraderie. Additionally, extracurricular activities, such as sports teams, clubs, and student organizations, offer valuable opportunities for students to connect with peers who share similar interests and passions.

Creating an inclusive environment is another critical aspect of fostering a sense of community in schools. Inclusivity means recognizing and celebrating the diverse backgrounds, cultures, and experiences of all students. Schools can promote inclusivity by incorporating diverse perspectives into the curriculum, celebrating cultural events and holidays, and ensuring that all students have access to the resources and support they need to succeed. When students see their identities and experiences reflected and valued in the school environment, they are more likely to feel a sense of belonging and connection.

Effective communication is essential for fostering a sense of community. Schools should establish clear and open lines of communication between students, teachers, parents, and administrators. This involves regularly sharing information about school events, policies, and achievements, as well as actively seeking input and feedback from all members of the school community. Transparent communication helps to build trust and ensures that everyone feels informed and involved. Schools can use various communication channels, such as newsletters, websites, social media, and meetings, to keep the community connected and engaged.

Parental and community involvement is also crucial for fostering a sense of community in schools. Parents and community members play an important role in supporting student learning and well-being. Schools can encourage parental involvement by providing opportunities for parents to participate in school activities, volunteer, and engage in decision-making processes. Community partnerships, such as collaborations with local businesses, organizations, and government agencies, can also provide valuable resources and support for the school. By involving parents and the broader community, schools can create a supportive network that enhances the sense of community and contributes to the overall success of students.

Mentorship programs are another effective way to foster a sense of community in schools. These programs pair students with mentors, who can be older students, teachers, or community members. Mentors provide guidance, support, and encouragement, helping mentees navigate academic and personal challenges. Mentorship programs build strong, supportive relationships that contribute to a sense of community and belonging. They also promote positive role modeling and help students develop important life skills.

Creating opportunities for student leadership and voice is essential for fostering a sense of community. When students have a say in decisions that affect their school experience, they feel more invested and connected to the school community. Schools can provide opportunities for student leadership through student councils, committees, and leadership programs. Additionally, schools should create spaces where students can share their ideas, concerns, and feedback, ensuring that their voices are heard and valued.

Building a sense of community also involves promoting social and emotional learning (SEL). SEL programs teach students skills such as self-awareness, self-regulation, empathy, and effective communication. These skills are essential for building positive relationships and creating a supportive school environment. SEL programs can be integrated into the curriculum through lessons, activities, and discussions that focus on social and emotional development. By prioritizing SEL, schools can help students develop the skills they need to contribute to a positive and inclusive community.

Celebrating achievements and milestones is another important aspect of fostering a sense of community. Recognizing and celebrating the accomplishments of students, teachers, and staff helps to build a positive school culture and reinforces the values of the school community. Celebrations can take various forms, such as award ceremonies, assemblies, newsletters, and social media shout-outs. By highlighting the successes of individuals and groups, schools can create a sense of pride and unity within the community.

Creating a safe and supportive environment is essential for fostering a sense of community in schools. Students need to feel safe, both physically and emotionally, to fully engage in the school community. Schools can promote safety by implementing clear policies and procedures for addressing bullying, harassment, and other negative behaviors.

Providing support services, such as counseling and mental health resources, is also crucial for ensuring that students have the help they need to navigate challenges and thrive. When students feel safe and supported, they are more likely to build positive relationships and contribute to a strong sense of community.

Professional development for teachers and staff is also important for fostering a sense of community. Educators need training and support to effectively build relationships, create inclusive environments, and promote social and emotional learning. Professional development opportunities can include workshops, seminars, and collaborative learning communities that focus on these topics. By investing in the professional growth of educators, schools can ensure that they have the skills and knowledge needed to foster a strong sense of community.

Reflective practice is another valuable tool for fostering a sense of community in schools. Reflective practice involves regularly examining one's actions, decisions, and interactions to gain insights and identify areas for improvement.

Educators can engage in reflective practice by keeping journals, participating in reflective discussions with colleagues, or setting aside time for personal contemplation. By reflecting on their efforts to build community, educators can learn from their experiences and develop strategies for enhancing the sense of community in their schools.

Fostering a sense of community in schools also involves addressing and overcoming barriers to inclusion and participation. Schools should identify and address any obstacles that may prevent students, teachers, or parents from fully engaging in the school community. This might include addressing issues related to language barriers, accessibility, socioeconomic disparities, and cultural differences. By actively working to remove these barriers, schools can create a more inclusive and welcoming environment for all members of the community.

Building a sense of community is an ongoing process that requires commitment and effort from everyone involved. Schools should regularly evaluate their efforts to foster community, seek feedback from students, parents, and staff, and make adjustments as needed. This continuous improvement process helps to ensure that the sense of community remains strong and responsive to the evolving needs of the school population.

Fostering a sense of community in schools is essential for creating an environment where students, teachers, and staff feel connected, supported, and valued. Building strong, positive relationships, creating an inclusive environment, and encouraging participation from all members of the school community are key strategies for achieving this goal.

Effective communication, parental and community involvement, mentorship programs, and opportunities for student leadership and voice are also important for fostering a sense of community. Promoting social and emotional learning, celebrating achievements, and creating a safe and supportive environment further enhance the sense of community. Professional development, reflective practice, and addressing barriers to inclusion are essential for sustaining and strengthening the sense of community in schools. By prioritizing these efforts, schools can create a positive and collaborative environment that supports the well-being and success of all students.

ppp

"The influence of family and community on ethical education is profound. Their values and behaviors shape the ethical frameworks of children. Schools must collaborate with these stakeholders to reinforce ethical principles."

ᚦᚦᚦ

SIXTEEN

ETHICS IN EDUCATIONAL POLICY AND ADMINISTRATION

Ethics in educational policy and administration is a cornerstone of creating fair, equitable, and effective learning environments. Ethical considerations must be integrated into all aspects of educational leadership to ensure that decisions, policies, and practices promote the well-being and success of all students. This integration requires a commitment to principles such as justice, fairness, integrity, transparency, and respect for all members of the educational community. Administrators and policymakers play a crucial role in shaping the ethical landscape of schools and educational institutions, influencing everything from resource allocation and discipline policies to curriculum development and stakeholder engagement.

One of the primary responsibilities of educational leaders is to ensure that policies and practices are fair and just. This involves creating an inclusive environment where all students, regardless of their background, have equal opportunities to succeed. Equity in education requires that resources are distributed in a way that addresses the diverse needs of students. For instance, schools in low-income areas may require additional funding to provide students with access to quality materials, technology, and support services. Ensuring that resource allocation is equitable rather than equal recognizes that different schools and students have different needs, and it is the ethical responsibility of policymakers to address these disparities.

Transparency is another critical aspect of ethical administration in education. Decision-making processes should be open and transparent to build trust and accountability. When administrators are transparent about how decisions are made, it fosters a sense of trust among students, parents, and staff. Transparency involves clear communication about policies, procedures, and the rationale behind decisions. This openness helps to prevent misunderstandings and promotes a collaborative environment where all stakeholders feel informed and involved.

Integrity is essential in educational policy and administration. Leaders must adhere to high ethical standards and demonstrate honesty in their actions and decisions. Integrity involves being consistent in applying rules and policies, ensuring that there are no double standards or favoritism. Administrators should also be willing to admit mistakes and take responsibility for their actions. This accountability builds credibility and sets a positive example for the entire school community. When leaders act with integrity, they reinforce the importance of ethical behavior and create a culture of trust and respect.

Respect for all individuals within the educational community is fundamental to ethical leadership. Policies and practices must be designed to uphold the dignity and rights of students, teachers, staff, and parents. This respect involves creating a safe and supportive environment where everyone feels valued and heard. Policies related to student discipline, for example, should be fair and consistent, focusing on restorative practices rather than punitive measures. This approach helps to address the root causes of behavior issues and supports the personal growth and development of students.

Ethical considerations also play a significant role in curriculum development and implementation. The curriculum should reflect the values and principles of the educational institution, promoting critical thinking, empathy, and social responsibility. It is essential to include diverse perspectives and materials that represent the experiences and contributions of different cultural, racial, and socioeconomic groups. This inclusivity helps students develop a broader understanding of the world and fosters a sense of belonging and respect for diversity. Ethical curriculum design also involves being mindful of the potential impact of content on students and ensuring that materials are appropriate and respectful.

Stakeholder engagement is another crucial aspect of ethical educational administration. Engaging students, parents, teachers, and the broader community in decision-making processes ensures that policies and practices reflect the needs and values of the entire educational community. This engagement can take many forms, such as advisory committees, public forums, surveys, and regular communication channels. By involving stakeholders in meaningful ways, administrators can build stronger relationships, foster a sense of shared responsibility, and enhance the effectiveness of educational policies and practices.

Professional development for educators and administrators is essential for promoting ethical practices in education. Continuous training on ethical issues, decision-making, and leadership helps to ensure that all members of the educational community are equipped to navigate complex ethical dilemmas. This professional development should include discussions on equity, diversity, inclusion, and the ethical use of technology and data. By prioritizing ongoing education on ethical issues, schools can create a culture of continuous improvement and ethical awareness.

Ethical leadership also involves advocating for policies that promote the well-being and success of all students. This advocacy might include pushing for increased funding for public education, supporting policies that address educational disparities, and promoting initiatives that enhance student health and safety. Administrators and policymakers have a responsibility to use their positions of influence to advocate for the needs of their students and to work towards systemic changes that benefit the educational community as a whole.

Data privacy and security are critical ethical considerations in educational policy and administration. With the increasing use of technology in education, protecting the privacy of students and staff is paramount. Policies must be in place to ensure that personal information is collected, stored, and used in ways that respect individuals' privacy rights. This involves implementing robust security measures to protect data from unauthorized access and ensuring that data is used ethically and transparently. Educators and administrators must be trained on data privacy issues and understand the ethical implications of their decisions related to technology and data use.

The ethical use of technology in education extends beyond data privacy. It also involves ensuring that all students have equitable access to technology and digital resources. The digital divide, where some students have limited access to technology due to socioeconomic factors, is a significant ethical issue that schools must address. Policies should be in place to provide necessary technology and support to students who need it, ensuring that all students have the tools they need to succeed in a digital learning environment.

Crisis management and ethical decision-making in times of crisis are also vital aspects of educational leadership. During crises, such as natural disasters, health emergencies, or social upheavals, administrators must make decisions that prioritize the safety and well-being of students and staff. These decisions often involve difficult ethical considerations, such as balancing the need for safety with the desire to maintain educational continuity. Transparent communication, stakeholder engagement, and adherence to ethical principles are essential during these times to ensure that decisions are made with the best interests of the community in mind.

Ethical leadership also requires a commitment to social justice and equity. This involves recognizing and addressing systemic inequities within the educational system and working towards creating a more just and equitable environment for all students. Policies should be designed to eliminate barriers to educational success and to support the needs of marginalized and underserved populations. This might include initiatives to improve access to advanced coursework, support for English language learners, and programs that address the social and emotional needs of students from diverse backgrounds.

Ethics in educational policy and administration is essential for creating fair, equitable, and effective learning environments. Ethical considerations must be integrated into all aspects of educational leadership, from resource allocation and curriculum development to stakeholder engagement and crisis management. Key principles such as fairness, transparency, integrity, respect, and social justice should guide the decisions and actions of administrators and policymakers. By fostering a culture of ethical awareness and continuous improvement, schools can ensure that their policies and practices promote the well-being and success of all students. Ethical leadership is not only about making the right decisions but also about creating an environment where everyone feels valued, respected, and empowered to achieve their full potential.

ᗘᗘᗘ

"Inclusivity and respect are the cornerstones of
ethical education. Every student deserves to feel
valued and supported. A culture of respect fosters
ethical behavior and positive relationships."

ÞÞÞ

SEVENTEEN

The Influence of Family and Community on Ethical Education

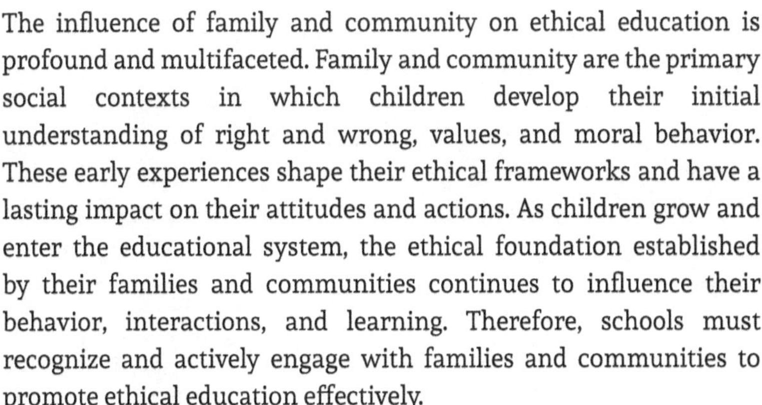

The influence of family and community on ethical education is profound and multifaceted. Family and community are the primary social contexts in which children develop their initial understanding of right and wrong, values, and moral behavior. These early experiences shape their ethical frameworks and have a lasting impact on their attitudes and actions. As children grow and enter the educational system, the ethical foundation established by their families and communities continues to influence their behavior, interactions, and learning. Therefore, schools must recognize and actively engage with families and communities to promote ethical education effectively.

Family is often the first and most influential context for ethical education. From a young age, children observe and internalize the values, beliefs, and behaviors of their parents and caregivers. Through everyday interactions, family members model ethical behavior, such as honesty, respect, responsibility, and compassion. These interactions provide children with concrete examples of how to navigate moral dilemmas and make ethical decisions. For instance, when parents demonstrate honesty by admitting mistakes or showing empathy by helping others in need, they teach their children the importance of these values.

Parental involvement in a child's education significantly enhances the ethical dimension of their learning. When parents engage with their children's schooling, they reinforce the ethical lessons taught in school and provide a consistent framework for moral development. This involvement can take various forms, including attending parent-teacher conferences, volunteering at school events, and discussing schoolwork and ethical issues at home. By being actively involved, parents show that they value education and ethical behavior, which encourages children to adopt similar attitudes.

Moreover, parents and caregivers play a crucial role in setting expectations and boundaries that guide their children's behavior. By establishing clear rules and consistent consequences, parents help children understand the importance of accountability and responsibility. For example, a family rule about completing homework before watching television teaches children the value of discipline and prioritizing responsibilities. Similarly, addressing unethical behavior, such as lying or cheating, with appropriate consequences reinforces the importance of honesty and integrity.

Open communication between parents and children is vital for ethical education. When parents create an environment where children feel comfortable discussing their thoughts, feelings, and ethical dilemmas, they provide valuable opportunities for moral reasoning and growth. These conversations help children develop critical thinking skills and learn to consider different perspectives and potential consequences of their actions. Parents can facilitate these discussions by asking open-ended questions, listening actively, and guiding their children through the process of ethical decision-making.

Community also plays a significant role in shaping children's ethical education. The broader social environment in which children live influences their values, attitudes, and behaviors. Community norms, cultural practices, and social interactions all contribute to the ethical framework that children develop. Schools, religious organizations, recreational clubs, and other community groups provide contexts where children learn and practice ethical behavior.

Schools are a central component of the community and serve as important settings for ethical education. Educators and school leaders must recognize the influence of family and community and actively engage with these stakeholders to create a cohesive and supportive environment for ethical learning. Collaborative partnerships between schools, families, and communities enhance the effectiveness of ethical education by providing consistent messages and reinforcing positive behaviors.

One way schools can engage with families and communities is by creating opportunities for involvement and collaboration. Schools can invite parents and community members to participate in school activities, such as mentoring programs, cultural events, and community service projects. These activities not only provide valuable learning experiences for students but also strengthen the connections between the school and the broader community. When students see their parents and community members actively involved in their education, they are more likely to value and adhere to the ethical principles being taught.

Community service and volunteer opportunities are particularly effective in promoting ethical education. When students participate in community service projects, they learn the importance of empathy, compassion, and social responsibility. These experiences help students understand the impact of their actions on others and develop a sense of civic duty. Schools can partner with local organizations to create meaningful service-learning opportunities that connect classroom learning with real-world ethical issues. By engaging in community service, students practice ethical behavior and contribute positively to their communities.

Religious and cultural organizations within the community also play a significant role in ethical education. These organizations often provide moral guidance and support, helping children develop a sense of identity and belonging. Religious teachings and cultural traditions can reinforce the values and principles taught at home and school, creating a cohesive framework for ethical development. Schools can collaborate with religious and cultural organizations to ensure that their ethical education programs are inclusive and respectful of diverse beliefs and practices.

Mentorship programs that involve community members can have a profound impact on students' ethical development. Mentors serve as role models, providing guidance, support, and positive examples of ethical behavior. These relationships help students develop trust, respect, and a sense of accountability. Mentorship programs can be particularly beneficial for at-risk students or those lacking strong family support, offering them additional sources of guidance and encouragement.

Involving students in decision-making processes within the school and community also promotes ethical education. When students have a voice in matters that affect them, they learn the importance of participation, responsibility, and ethical leadership. Schools can create student councils, advisory committees, and other platforms where students can contribute their ideas and opinions. This involvement empowers students and helps them develop critical thinking and ethical decision-making skills.

Community-wide initiatives that promote ethical behavior and values can have a significant impact on students. Programs that address issues such as bullying, substance abuse, and violence prevention create a supportive environment where ethical behavior is encouraged and reinforced. Schools can collaborate with local government agencies, non-profit organizations, and businesses to implement these initiatives and provide resources and support for students and families.

The media also plays a role in shaping children's ethical education. Television, movies, social media, and other forms of media influence children's perceptions of right and wrong, as well as their understanding of social norms and values. Parents, educators, and community leaders must guide children in critically analyzing media messages and understanding their ethical implications. Media literacy programs can help students develop the skills to discern and evaluate the ethical dimensions of the content they consume.

Ultimately, the combined influence of family and community creates a comprehensive support system for ethical education. When families, schools, and communities work together, they create a consistent and reinforcing environment that promotes ethical behavior and values. This collaboration ensures that children receive clear and consistent messages about the importance of ethics, both in their personal lives and as members of society.

To maximize the impact of family and community on ethical education, schools must prioritize building strong partnerships with these stakeholders. This requires ongoing communication, mutual respect, and a shared commitment to the well-being and success of students. By fostering these partnerships, schools can create a supportive and inclusive environment that nurtures the ethical development of all students.

The influence of family and community on ethical education is profound and essential for the holistic development of children. Families provide the foundational values and behaviors that shape children's ethical frameworks, while communities offer diverse opportunities for practicing and reinforcing these principles. Schools play a crucial role in integrating and amplifying these influences through collaborative partnerships and inclusive practices. By recognizing and leveraging the combined impact of family and community, schools can effectively promote ethical education and prepare students to navigate the complexities of the modern world with integrity and compassion.

ᚦᚦᚦ

"Ethical excellence in education is built on a foundation of trust. Trust between educators, students, and the community is essential. Transparency and honesty are key to maintaining this trust."

❥❥❥

EIGHTEEN

TECHNOLOGY AND ETHICS: NAVIGATING THE DIGITAL AGE

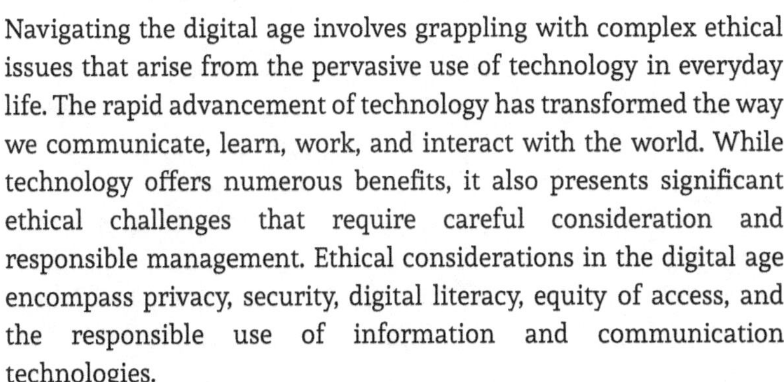

Navigating the digital age involves grappling with complex ethical issues that arise from the pervasive use of technology in everyday life. The rapid advancement of technology has transformed the way we communicate, learn, work, and interact with the world. While technology offers numerous benefits, it also presents significant ethical challenges that require careful consideration and responsible management. Ethical considerations in the digital age encompass privacy, security, digital literacy, equity of access, and the responsible use of information and communication technologies.

Privacy is one of the foremost ethical concerns in the digital age. The collection, storage, and use of personal data by various entities, including corporations, governments, and educational institutions, raise questions about individuals' rights to privacy. Personal data can include sensitive information such as health records, financial details, and online activities. The ethical issue lies in how this data is collected, who has access to it, and how it is used. Organizations must ensure that they handle personal data with the utmost care, implementing robust data protection measures and respecting individuals' privacy rights. This involves being transparent about data collection practices, obtaining informed consent from individuals, and providing them with control over their personal information.

Security is closely related to privacy and is another critical ethical concern in the digital age. Cybersecurity threats, such as hacking, phishing, and malware, pose significant risks to individuals and organizations. Ethical considerations in cybersecurity involve protecting sensitive information from unauthorized access and ensuring the integrity and availability of data. Organizations must invest in robust security measures, such as encryption, firewalls, and regular security audits, to safeguard against cyber threats. Additionally, they must educate users about safe online practices and the importance of protecting their personal information.

Digital literacy is essential for navigating the ethical challenges of the digital age. Digital literacy involves the ability to use technology effectively and responsibly, understand the ethical implications of digital actions, and critically evaluate digital content. Educators play a crucial role in fostering digital literacy among students, equipping them with the skills and knowledge needed to navigate the digital world ethically. This includes teaching students about online privacy, cybersecurity, digital citizenship, and the ethical use of information and communication technologies. By promoting digital literacy, educators help students become informed and responsible digital citizens who can make ethical decisions in the digital realm.

Equity of access is another significant ethical issue in the digital age. The digital divide refers to the gap between individuals who have access to modern information and communication technologies and those who do not. This divide can exacerbate existing social inequalities, as individuals without access to technology may face disadvantages in education, employment, and social participation. Ensuring equitable access to technology is an ethical imperative, requiring efforts to provide affordable and reliable internet access, digital devices, and digital literacy training to underserved populations. Schools and governments play a critical role in bridging the digital divide by implementing policies and programs that promote digital inclusion and ensure that all individuals have the opportunity to benefit from technological advancements.

The responsible use of information and communication technologies is a key ethical consideration in the digital age. This involves using technology in ways that are respectful, fair, and beneficial to society. Ethical technology use includes respecting intellectual property rights, avoiding plagiarism, and giving proper credit to the creators of digital content. It also involves using technology to promote positive social interactions, such as fostering respectful and inclusive online communities, and avoiding behaviors that can cause harm, such as cyberbullying, harassment, and the spread of misinformation. Educators and parents play a crucial role in guiding young people in the responsible use of technology, setting clear expectations and modeling ethical behavior.

The rise of social media has brought about new ethical challenges related to communication and information sharing. Social media platforms can be powerful tools for connecting people, sharing information, and promoting social causes. However, they can also be used to spread misinformation, invade privacy, and perpetuate harmful behaviors. Ethical considerations in social media use include verifying the accuracy of information before sharing it, respecting the privacy of others, and engaging in respectful and constructive online interactions. Social media users must be aware of the potential impact of their actions and take responsibility for their online behavior.

Artificial intelligence (AI) and machine learning present additional ethical challenges in the digital age. These technologies have the potential to revolutionize various fields, from healthcare to education, but they also raise important ethical questions. Issues such as bias in AI algorithms, the transparency of AI decision-making processes, and the potential for job displacement due to automation are all areas of concern. Ethical AI development involves ensuring that AI systems are designed and used in ways that are fair, transparent, and accountable. This includes addressing biases in data and algorithms, providing explanations for AI decisions, and considering the broader social implications of AI technologies.

The ethical use of technology in education is a critical area of focus. Educational institutions must navigate the balance between leveraging technology to enhance learning and ensuring that its use is ethical and equitable. This includes protecting student privacy, ensuring that digital learning tools are accessible to all students, and using technology in ways that support rather than replace meaningful human interactions. Educators must also be mindful of the potential for technology to distract or disengage students and strive to integrate technology in ways that genuinely enhance the learning experience.

Ethical considerations also extend to the development and implementation of new technologies. Innovators and developers must consider the potential ethical implications of their creations from the outset, ensuring that new technologies are designed and used in ways that benefit society and minimize harm. This involves conducting ethical impact assessments, seeking input from diverse stakeholders, and adhering to principles such as fairness, accountability, and transparency. By prioritizing ethical considerations in the development process, technologists can create innovations that contribute positively to society.

The role of regulation and policy in addressing ethical issues in the digital age is also critical. Governments and regulatory bodies must establish and enforce laws and regulations that protect individuals' rights and promote ethical behavior. This includes regulations related to data privacy, cybersecurity, digital content, and AI. Policymakers must stay informed about technological advancements and their potential ethical implications, ensuring that regulations keep pace with innovation and address emerging challenges. Collaboration between governments, industry, and civil society is essential for developing effective policies that balance the benefits and risks of technology.

In the workplace, ethical considerations related to technology include issues such as employee monitoring, data privacy, and the impact of automation on jobs. Employers must navigate the balance between using technology to enhance productivity and respecting employees' privacy and rights. This involves implementing clear policies on the use of technology, ensuring transparency about data collection and monitoring practices, and considering the ethical implications of automation and AI in the workplace. Ethical considerations in the workplace also include providing employees with training and support to navigate the digital landscape responsibly.

Finally, fostering a culture of ethical technology use requires education, awareness, and a commitment to ethical principles at all levels of society. Schools, businesses, governments, and individuals all have a role to play in promoting ethical behavior in the digital age. This involves ongoing education and training on ethical issues related to technology, creating policies and practices that promote ethical behavior, and holding individuals and organizations accountable for their actions. By prioritizing ethics in the digital age, we can harness the benefits of technology while mitigating its risks and ensuring that it is used in ways that promote the well-being of all.

Navigating the digital age requires careful consideration of the ethical challenges that arise from the pervasive use of technology. Privacy, security, digital literacy, equity of access, and responsible use are all critical ethical considerations. Addressing these challenges involves fostering digital literacy, ensuring equitable access to technology, promoting responsible use, and considering the ethical implications of new technologies. Collaboration between governments, industry, and civil society is essential for developing effective policies and regulations that promote ethical behavior. By prioritizing ethics in the digital age, we can create a technological landscape that benefits society and respects the rights and well-being of all individuals.

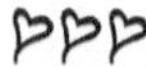

"Schools play a crucial role in preparing students for ethical challenges in the digital age. Teaching digital ethics is part of this responsibility. Students must learn to navigate the online world with integrity."

➤➤➤

NINETEEN

Case Studies: Real-Life Examples of Ethical Excellence in Education

Ethical excellence in education is best illustrated through real-life examples, where educators and institutions have faced ethical challenges and responded in ways that uphold the highest standards of integrity, fairness, and respect. These case studies not only highlight the impact of ethical decision-making on students and the broader school community but also serve as models for others to follow. By examining these examples, we can gain insights into the principles and practices that contribute to ethical excellence in education.

One notable example of ethical excellence in education is the case of a high school principal who took a stand against systemic inequities in her school. Faced with a significant achievement gap between students from different socioeconomic backgrounds, she implemented a comprehensive strategy to address these disparities. This strategy included reallocating resources to provide additional support for underserved students, such as tutoring, mentoring, and access to advanced coursework. She also advocated for professional development focused on culturally responsive teaching practices to help teachers better understand and meet the needs of diverse learners. Through her leadership and commitment to equity, the principal not only improved academic outcomes for disadvantaged students but also fostered a more inclusive and supportive school environment.

Another example involves a group of teachers at an elementary school who collaborated to create a restorative justice program to address disciplinary issues. Recognizing that traditional punitive approaches to discipline often failed to address the root causes of behavior problems and disproportionately affected minority students, these teachers sought an alternative approach. They developed a program that focused on repairing harm, fostering accountability, and rebuilding relationships. This program included restorative circles, mediation sessions, and opportunities for students to make amends. By implementing restorative justice practices, the teachers reduced suspension rates, improved student behavior, and created a more positive and respectful school culture.

A third case study highlights the ethical leadership of a university professor who championed academic integrity in her institution. Concerned about the prevalence of plagiarism and cheating, she led an initiative to promote a culture of honesty and integrity among students and faculty. This initiative included revising the university's academic integrity policy, providing training and resources for faculty on how to detect and address academic misconduct, and launching a student-led honor code. She also organized workshops and seminars to educate students about the importance of academic integrity and the consequences of unethical behavior. Through her efforts, the professor significantly reduced instances of academic dishonesty and fostered a culture of trust and integrity within the university.

An inspiring example of ethical excellence in education can be seen in the efforts of a school district superintendent who prioritized the mental health and well-being of students and staff. In response to rising concerns about stress, anxiety, and mental health issues among students, the superintendent implemented a comprehensive mental health program. This program included hiring additional school counselors, providing mental health training for teachers and staff, and creating partnerships with local mental health organizations to offer on-site services. The superintendent also promoted a balanced approach to education, emphasizing the importance of social-emotional learning and reducing unnecessary academic pressures. As a result, the district saw improvements in student well-being, reduced absenteeism, and a more supportive and compassionate school environment.

A further example of ethical excellence involves a middle school teacher who integrated ethical discussions into her science curriculum. Recognizing the importance of teaching students to think critically about the ethical implications of scientific advancements, she designed lessons that explored topics such as genetic engineering, environmental sustainability, and medical ethics. She encouraged students to consider different perspectives, engage in debates, and reflect on their own values. By incorporating ethical considerations into her teaching, the teacher helped students develop a deeper understanding of the complex relationship between science and society and fostered their ability to make informed and ethical decisions.

Another powerful example is the case of a high school counselor who implemented a comprehensive college access program for first-generation and low-income students. Understanding the barriers these students faced in accessing higher education, the counselor provided personalized guidance and support throughout the college application process. This support included helping students research colleges, prepare for standardized tests, complete applications, and apply for financial aid. The counselor also organized college visits and workshops to provide students with additional resources and information. Through her dedication and advocacy, the counselor significantly increased the number of first-generation and low-income students who were accepted to and enrolled in college, demonstrating the impact of ethical commitment to educational equity.

A university president's response to a campus-wide crisis involving allegations of sexual misconduct also exemplifies ethical excellence in education. Faced with a situation that required immediate and decisive action, the president prioritized transparency, accountability, and support for survivors. She established an independent task force to investigate the allegations, implemented new policies to prevent future incidents, and provided comprehensive support services for survivors, including counseling and legal assistance. The president also led campus-wide initiatives to promote a culture of respect and consent, including mandatory training for all students and staff. By taking a proactive and ethical approach, the president not only addressed the immediate crisis but also worked to create a safer and more respectful campus environment.

An additional example can be found in the actions of a charter school director who faced pressure to exclude students with disabilities to improve the school's performance metrics. The director refused to compromise her ethical principles and instead focused on creating an inclusive environment that supported all students. She implemented targeted interventions and support services for students with disabilities, such as individualized education plans (IEPs), specialized instructional strategies, and assistive technologies. The director also provided professional development for teachers on inclusive teaching practices. Her commitment to inclusion not only upheld the rights of students with disabilities but also demonstrated that educational excellence can be achieved through ethical and equitable practices.

The ethical leadership of a school board member who advocated for the integration of ethics education into the district's curriculum offers another compelling case study. Believing that ethical education was essential for developing responsible and engaged citizens, the board member worked to secure funding and support for a comprehensive ethics education program. This program included ethics courses, interdisciplinary projects that incorporated ethical discussions, and extracurricular activities focused on ethical issues. The board member also collaborated with local businesses and community organizations to provide real-world learning opportunities for students. Through her efforts, the district developed a robust ethics education program that empowered students to think critically about ethical dilemmas and make principled decisions.

Finally, a notable example of ethical excellence in education can be seen in the response of a school principal to a community crisis. When a natural disaster struck the community, the principal mobilized the school to serve as a hub for relief efforts. She coordinated with local agencies to provide shelter, food, and medical care for affected families. The principal also organized a fundraising campaign to support rebuilding efforts and ensured that students had access to counseling and support services to cope with the trauma. Her leadership during the crisis demonstrated a deep commitment to the well-being of the entire community and highlighted the role of schools as centers of support and resilience.

These case studies illustrate the transformative impact of ethical excellence in education. Educators and leaders who prioritize ethical principles create positive, inclusive, and supportive environments that benefit students, staff, and the broader community. Through their actions, they demonstrate that ethical decision-making is not only the right thing to do but also a powerful catalyst for positive change. These examples serve as valuable models for others in the field of education, inspiring a commitment to ethical excellence and highlighting the profound difference that ethical leadership can make. By learning from these real-life examples, educators and institutions can continue to strive for ethical excellence, ensuring that their decisions and actions contribute to the well-being and success of all students.

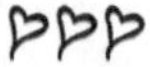

"Effective ethical leadership requires courage and commitment. Leaders must address ethical dilemmas head-on and provide clear guidance. Their example sets the standard for the entire school community."

❥❥❥

TWENTY

THE PATH FORWARD FOR ETHICAL EXCELLENCE IN EDUCATION

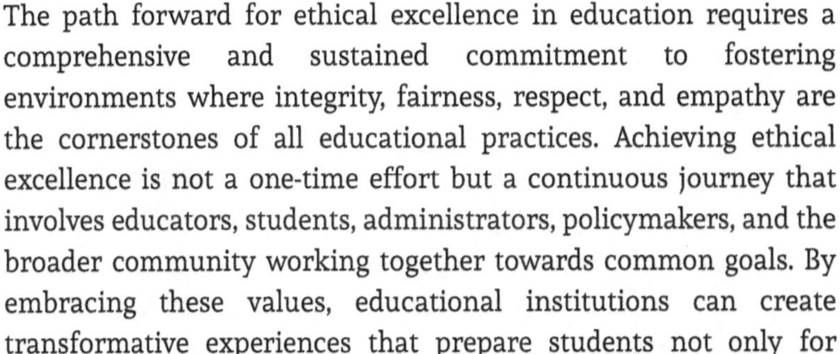

The path forward for ethical excellence in education requires a comprehensive and sustained commitment to fostering environments where integrity, fairness, respect, and empathy are the cornerstones of all educational practices. Achieving ethical excellence is not a one-time effort but a continuous journey that involves educators, students, administrators, policymakers, and the broader community working together towards common goals. By embracing these values, educational institutions can create transformative experiences that prepare students not only for academic success but also for ethical and responsible citizenship.

At the heart of ethical excellence in education is the recognition that every decision and action taken within the educational system has ethical implications. This awareness necessitates a deliberate and reflective approach to decision-making, ensuring that all policies and practices are aligned with core ethical principles. Educators and administrators must consistently ask themselves how their actions affect students' well-being, equity, and justice. This reflective practice helps to maintain a focus on what is truly important: the development of students as whole individuals who are capable of making positive contributions to society.

To foster ethical excellence, it is crucial to embed ethical education within the curriculum. This involves not only teaching about ethics as a standalone subject but integrating ethical discussions and considerations into all areas of learning. By doing so, students learn to apply ethical reasoning in various contexts, whether in science, literature, history, or mathematics. This interdisciplinary approach helps students understand that ethical thinking is not confined to certain subjects but is a fundamental aspect of all knowledge and human interaction. Educators can facilitate this by creating opportunities for students to engage with real-world ethical dilemmas, encouraging critical thinking, debate, and reflection.

The role of educators in modeling ethical behavior cannot be overstated. Teachers and administrators must exemplify the values they wish to instill in their students. This includes demonstrating integrity, fairness, respect, and empathy in their interactions with students and colleagues. By acting as role models, educators can significantly influence students' moral development. It is essential for educators to be transparent, admit mistakes, and show a commitment to continuous improvement. This openness fosters a culture of trust and respect, where ethical behavior is seen as a collective responsibility.

Professional development is a key component in achieving ethical excellence in education. Educators need ongoing training and support to effectively integrate ethical principles into their teaching and leadership practices. Professional development programs should focus on ethical theories, case studies, and practical strategies for addressing ethical dilemmas. These programs can also provide a platform for educators to share experiences and best practices, fostering a collaborative approach to ethical education. By investing in the professional growth of educators, schools can ensure that their staff are well-equipped to navigate the complex ethical challenges they encounter.

The involvement of parents and the broader community is also critical in promoting ethical excellence. Schools should actively seek to engage parents in the educational process, recognizing them as partners in their children's ethical development. This can be achieved through regular communication, workshops, and opportunities for parents to participate in school activities. Community involvement can extend to partnerships with local organizations, businesses, and cultural institutions, providing students with diverse perspectives and experiences. By building strong connections between the school and the community, students receive consistent messages about the importance of ethical behavior and social responsibility.

Creating an inclusive and equitable school environment is fundamental to ethical excellence. This involves recognizing and addressing the diverse needs of all students, ensuring that everyone has equal opportunities to succeed. Schools must implement policies and practices that promote inclusivity, such as differentiated instruction, support services for students with disabilities, and programs that address the needs of marginalized groups. An inclusive environment fosters a sense of belonging and respect, which are essential for ethical development. When students feel valued and supported, they are more likely to engage positively with their education and contribute to a positive school culture.

Technology plays a significant role in modern education, and its ethical use is a critical consideration. Schools must ensure that technology is used in ways that enhance learning and respect students' privacy and rights. This includes implementing robust data protection measures, promoting digital literacy, and teaching students about the ethical implications of their online behavior. Educators should guide students in understanding the impact of technology on society and encourage them to use digital tools responsibly. By addressing the ethical challenges associated with technology, schools can prepare students to navigate the digital world with integrity.

Ethical leadership is essential for driving the pursuit of ethical excellence in education. School leaders must prioritize ethical considerations in all aspects of their decision-making and create a culture that values ethical behavior. This involves setting clear expectations, providing support and resources for ethical practices, and holding everyone accountable to high ethical standards. Leaders should also be advocates for policies that promote equity and justice within the educational system. By demonstrating ethical leadership, school administrators can inspire and motivate others to uphold the same values.

Assessment and accountability are important components of ethical excellence. Schools should establish mechanisms to regularly evaluate their ethical practices and ensure that they are meeting their goals. This can include self-assessment tools, external reviews, and feedback from students, parents, and staff. By continuously monitoring and improving their ethical practices, schools can remain responsive to the evolving needs of their community and maintain high standards of integrity.

Finally, fostering a sense of community within schools is vital for ethical excellence. A strong sense of community encourages collaboration, mutual support, and shared responsibility. Schools can build community through activities that bring people together, such as school events, service projects, and collaborative learning experiences. By creating a supportive and inclusive community, schools can provide a foundation for ethical behavior and help students develop the social and emotional skills needed to thrive.

The path forward for ethical excellence in education requires a holistic and sustained effort from all members of the educational community. By integrating ethical principles into the curriculum, modeling ethical behavior, investing in professional development, engaging parents and the community, creating inclusive environments, responsibly using technology, demonstrating ethical leadership, ensuring accountability, and fostering a sense of community, schools can create environments where ethical excellence thrives. This commitment to ethics not only enhances the educational experience but also prepares students to become responsible and engaged citizens who contribute positively to society. Through these efforts, we can build a future where ethical excellence is the norm in education, benefiting individuals and the broader community alike.

"The journey towards ethical excellence is a shared responsibility. It involves educators, students, parents, and community members. Together, we can create an educational environment that values and promotes ethical behavior."

ᗡᗡᗡ

TWENTY-ONE
SUMMARY

The journey towards ethical excellence in education is an ongoing and multifaceted process that involves the collective efforts of educators, students, administrators, policymakers, parents, and the broader community. This comprehensive approach to ethics in education is essential for creating environments that foster integrity, fairness, respect, and empathy, ultimately preparing students for both academic success and responsible citizenship.

The foundation of ethical excellence in education lies in the integration of ethical principles into all aspects of the educational system. This begins with establishing clear ethical frameworks that guide decision-making and ensure that policies and practices are aligned with core values. Educators and administrators must consistently reflect on how their actions affect students' well-being, equity, and justice. This reflective practice helps maintain a focus on the holistic development of students, encouraging them to think critically and act ethically in various contexts.

Ethical education should be embedded within the curriculum, not as a standalone subject but as an integral part of all learning areas. This interdisciplinary approach helps students understand that ethical thinking is fundamental to all knowledge and human interaction. By incorporating ethical discussions and real-world dilemmas into subjects such as science, literature, history, and mathematics, educators can foster critical thinking and ethical reasoning. This method ensures that students are well-equipped to navigate complex ethical issues in their personal and professional lives.

Educators play a crucial role in modeling ethical behavior. Teachers and administrators must exemplify values such as integrity, fairness, respect, and empathy in their interactions with students and colleagues. Acting as role models, they can significantly influence students' moral development. Transparency, accountability, and a commitment to continuous improvement are essential traits for educators to demonstrate. This openness fosters a culture of trust and respect, where ethical behavior is a shared responsibility among all members of the school community.

Professional development is vital for promoting ethical practices in education. Educators need ongoing training and support to effectively integrate ethical principles into their teaching and leadership practices. Professional development programs should focus on ethical theories, case studies, and practical strategies for addressing ethical dilemmas. By investing in the professional growth of educators, schools can ensure that their staff are well-prepared to handle the ethical challenges they encounter.

Parental and community involvement is critical in supporting ethical education. Schools should actively engage parents in the educational process, recognizing them as partners in their children's ethical development. This involvement can take various forms, such as attending school events, participating in workshops, and contributing to decision-making processes. Community partnerships with local organizations, businesses, and cultural institutions can provide students with diverse perspectives and experiences, reinforcing the importance of ethical behavior and social responsibility.

Creating an inclusive and equitable school environment is fundamental to ethical excellence. Schools must recognize and address the diverse needs of all students, ensuring equal opportunities for success. Implementing policies and practices that promote inclusivity, such as differentiated instruction and support services for students with disabilities, fosters a sense of belonging and respect. When students feel valued and supported, they are more likely to engage positively with their education and contribute to a positive school culture.

The ethical use of technology is a critical consideration in modern education. Schools must ensure that technology enhances learning while respecting students' privacy and rights. This involves implementing robust data protection measures, promoting digital literacy, and teaching students about the ethical implications of their online behavior. Educators should guide students in understanding the impact of technology on society and encourage them to use digital tools responsibly. Addressing these ethical challenges prepares students to navigate the digital world with integrity.

Ethical leadership is essential for driving the pursuit of ethical excellence in education. School leaders must prioritize ethical considerations in all aspects of their decision-making and create a culture that values ethical behavior. This involves setting clear expectations, providing support and resources for ethical practices, and holding everyone accountable to high ethical standards. Leaders should advocate for policies that promote equity and justice within the educational system, inspiring others to uphold the same values.

Assessment and accountability are important components of ethical excellence. Schools should establish mechanisms to regularly evaluate their ethical practices and ensure that they are meeting their goals. This can include self-assessment tools, external reviews, and feedback from students, parents, and staff. Continuous monitoring and improvement help schools remain responsive to the evolving needs of their community and maintain high standards of integrity.

Fostering a sense of community within schools is vital for ethical excellence. A strong sense of community encourages collaboration, mutual support, and shared responsibility. Schools can build community through activities that bring people together, such as school events, service projects, and collaborative learning experiences. Creating a supportive and inclusive community provides a foundation for ethical behavior and helps students develop the social and emotional skills needed to thrive.

Real-life examples of ethical excellence in education highlight the transformative impact of ethical decision-making on students and the broader school community. These case studies illustrate how educators and institutions have faced ethical challenges and responded in ways that uphold the highest standards of integrity, fairness, and respect. For instance, a high school principal addressing systemic inequities, teachers implementing restorative justice programs, and university professors promoting academic integrity all demonstrate the power of ethical leadership and commitment.

The influence of family and community on ethical education is profound. Family and community are the primary social contexts in which children develop their initial understanding of right and wrong, values, and moral behavior. Schools must recognize and actively engage with families and communities to promote ethical education effectively. By creating strong partnerships with these stakeholders, schools can provide a consistent and reinforcing environment that supports ethical behavior and values.

In the digital age, ethical considerations encompass privacy, security, digital literacy, equity of access, and responsible use of technology. Navigating these challenges involves fostering digital literacy, ensuring equitable access to technology, and promoting responsible use. Collaboration between governments, industry, and civil society is essential for developing effective policies and regulations that promote ethical behavior. By prioritizing ethics in the digital age, we can create a technological landscape that benefits society and respects the rights and well-being of all individuals.

The path forward for ethical excellence in education requires a holistic and sustained effort from all members of the educational community. By integrating ethical principles into the curriculum, modeling ethical behavior, investing in professional development, engaging parents and the community, creating inclusive environments, responsibly using technology, demonstrating ethical leadership, ensuring accountability, and fostering a sense of community, schools can create environments where ethical excellence thrives. This commitment to ethics not only enhances the educational experience but also prepares students to become responsible and engaged citizens who contribute positively to society. Through these efforts, we can build a future where ethical excellence is the norm in education, benefiting individuals and the broader community alike.

Ethical excellence in education is a continuous journey that involves the collective efforts of educators, students, administrators, policymakers, parents, and the broader community. By embracing values such as integrity, fairness, respect, and empathy, educational institutions can create transformative experiences that prepare students for both academic success and responsible citizenship. This comprehensive approach to ethics in education is essential for creating environments that foster the holistic development of students and ensure that they are well-equipped to navigate the complexities of the modern world with integrity and compassion.

Through the commitment to ethical excellence, we can create a brighter future for all, where education serves as a powerful force for positive change in society.

ϼϼϼ

Citation And References

This book represents the culmination of extensive research and meticulous analysis, incorporating a diverse range of sources, including numerous books, scholarly studies, and personal experiences. Additionally, I have scoured various websites to gather relevant information and data essential for the compilation of this work. I have taken every precaution to ensure the accuracy of the information presented and have diligently cited all sources to acknowledge their contributions.

Despite these efforts, the possibility of inadvertent errors remains. I deeply value the insights of my readers and appreciate any feedback that can help identify and rectify such inaccuracies. I encourage you to bring any discrepancies to my attention.

Your feedback is not only welcome but crucial, as it will aid in correcting current editions and enhancing the content of future ones. I am committed to maintaining the highest standards of accuracy and reliability in my work and thank you for your support and understanding.

Additionally, I firmly uphold the principle of freedom of speech and expression as guaranteed under Article 19(1)(a) of the Constitution of India, and I respect the diverse viewpoints and expressions of all readers.

ᏜᏜᏜ

Other Books Of The Author

1. Empowering Minds: A Journey into Women's Self-Discovery and Power
2. The Dynamics of Motivation: Catalyzing Thought into Action
3. Meditation and Mental Well Being: The Path to Inner Peace and Clarity
4. The Psychology of Child Education: Nurturing Future Generations
5. Ethical Enlightenment: A Modern Guide to Living with Integrity
6. Voices of Empowerment: Stories of Women Rising Against Odds
7. Social Psychology in Everyday Life: Understanding Human Connections
8. The Essence of Motivational Speaking: Inspiring Change in Others
9. Balancing Acts: Women, Work, and the Will to Lead
10. Guiding with Grace: Raising Children with Compassion and Awareness
11. The Power of Positive Aging: Embracing Life After Fifty
12. Building Resilient Communities: Social Work in Action
13. The Ethical Educator: Principles for Teaching and Learning
14. From Insight to Impact: Social Psychology for a Better World
15. The Ethics of Empathy: A Guide to Ethical Living
16. The Science of Empowering the Self: Navigating Life's Challenges with Psychological Wisdom
17. The Mindful Conscious Leader: Meditation Techniques for Modern Management
18. Pioneering Spirit: Women's Pathways to Leadership and Empowerment
19. Feeling to Healing: The Role of Emotional Intelligence in Child Development
20. Transformative Talks and Words of Inspiration: Insights into Motivational Oratory

21. Green Ethics: A Path to Sustainable Living
22. Spiritual Integrity: Navigating Life with Moral Compassion
23. Clean Living, Clean Society: The Ethics of Cleanliness
24. Patriotic Spirits: Building a Nation on Positive Attitudes
25. Innovative Integrity & Vibrant Visions: The Ethical and Entrepreneurial Spirit of Gujarat
26. Youthful Visions, Endless Possibilities: Inspiring Ethics and Motivation in Children
27. Living Your Legacy: How to Motivate Others by Living Your Values
28. Secret of Healing Conversations: Ethical Practices in Counselling and Therapy
29. Creative Kindness: Crafting a Life of Compassion and Creativity
30. The Power of Appreciation: How Gratitude Can Transform Your Relationships
31. Bhagavad-Gita: Messages
32. Science of Art: The New Frontier of Fashion Modernism
33. Vivekananda's Virtues: A Blueprint for Modern Living
34. Empower Her: Navigating the Path to Women's Entrepreneurship
35. The Boundless Classroom: Innovations in Global Education
36. The Language of Leadership: Communicating with Authenticity and Impact
37. The Warrior's Mantra: Deciphering the Hanuman Chalisa
38. Echoes of Empathy: Transformative Stories of Social Service
39. Artful Living: Cultivating Creativity in Your Daily Routine
40. Finding Your Why: Discovering Your Passions and Charting Your Course
41. The Role of Social Media in Shaping Self-Esteem and Interpersonal Relationships among Adolescents
42. Karma's Tapestry: Weaving a Life of Selfless Service
43. Altruistic Alchemy: Transforming Lives Through Giving
44. The Blueprint of Pro-Activeness and Productivity: Crafting Habits for Success
45. The Simplicity with Grounded Wisdom: Embracing Authenticity

Bhajan

101.   Pilgrimage of the Soul: Spiritual Journeys in India

ৡৡৡ

Contact

Dr. Minakshi Bansal
Social Activist
Ahmedabad, Gujarat, Bharat
minakshiindiag20@yahoo.com

ꕥꕥꕥ

|| LOKAHA SAMASTHAHA SUKHINO BHAVANTU ||